Consciousness Becomes You

Consciousness Becomes You

Angie Aristone & Roderick Alan

6th BOOKS

Winchester, UK
Washington, USA

First published by Sixth Books, 2016
Sixth Books is an imprint of John Hunt Publishing Ltd., Laurel House, Station Approach,
Alresford, Hants, SO24 9JH, UK
office1@jhpbooks.net
www.johnhuntpublishing.com
www.6th-books.com

For distributor details and how to order please visit the 'Ordering' section on our website.

ISBN: 978 1 78535 133 4
978 1 78535 134 1 (ebook)
Library of Congress Control Number: 2016935251

A CIP catalogue record for this book is available from the British Library.

Design: Stuart Davies

Printed and bound by CPI Group (UK) Ltd, Croydon, CR0 4YY, UK

CONTENTS

Part I – Unlearning **1**
Preface 2
Introduction 5
Leaving the Dark Ages 18
A No Brainer 37
Fear, Magic and a Second Level of Reality 48
Thinking Outside of the Brain 64
The Synergetic Effect 80
What Words Can't Express 105

Part II – The Connected Mind **117**
The Survivor Mind – A Toolbox for Physical Reality 118
The Connected Mind 130
It's About Time – All Mushed Up 152
Subtle Realities – Whose Thought Is It Anyway? 161
Playing in Subtle Reality... Spontaneous Knowing and Telepathic Networks 172
Tours of (Personal) Subtle Reality 197
Win-Win-Win Changes Everything 206
Epilogue – Telepathic Conversations 216

Notes 241

For Leslie. Our time together was far too short. Words can't begin to express the love and gratitude I feel for your constant presence and wise influence in my life... and thank you for turning my life around at 21. Your message was loud and clear.

Part I – Unlearning

Preface

Four blind men were led to an elephant...

"An elephant is like a column," said the first blind man, hugging the elephant's leg.

"Nooo, an elephant is like a fan," exclaimed the second blind man, flapping the elephant's ear.

"No, noooo, an elephant is like a spear," yelled the third blind man, caressing the elephant's tusk.

"No, noo, noo, noooo, noooo! An elephant is like a rope," sighed the fourth blind man, wiggling the elephant's trunk.

~ Ancient Proverb

This book is written from the perspective of a proverbial blind woman with her hand on the elephant; not to argue over what the elephant is, but to share what I've found, and help you put your hand on the elephant too. Though I humbly share what I've found, and acknowledge that there are many parts of the metaphorical elephant I haven't put my hand on yet, I must fiercely insist that the elephant is very real, and there for everyone to experience – if you are willing to try.

What follows is a perspective based on my personal experiences, and the product of many long conversations between my partner and I to reconcile my experiences with modern life, science, religion, shamanic traditions and new age teachings. Although this book is written mostly first person from my perspective, it is the product of a joint effort and you will notice the ebb and flow of both our voices throughout this guide. True to the subject matter, we wrote this book in connected states and ways in which far more was accomplished together than either of us could have managed alone. In writing the book, it became impossible for us to separate our contributions, or our voices.

In sharing this work we hope to help you understand and

embrace an essential, sacred and powerful part of yourself and others; a part of all of us that you may be uncomfortable with, as it has been ridiculed, objectified, demonized and denied by mainstream culture for centuries. In doing so, we hope to give you access to a whole new realm of connection, meaning, extra-ordinary experience, empowerment and possibility.

A human being is a part of the whole called by us universe, a part limited in time and space. He experiences himself, his thoughts and feeling as something separated from the rest, a kind of optical delusion of his consciousness. This delusion is a kind of prison for us, restricting us to our personal desires and to affection for a few persons nearest to us. Our task must be to free ourselves from this prison by widening our circle of compassion to embrace all living creatures and the whole of nature in its beauty.
~ Albert Einstein

Introduction

And those who were seen dancing were thought to be insane by those who could not hear the music.
~ Nietzsche

People often ask me about my childhood, I think, because they want to know if you can learn to be telepathic, or if you have to be born that way. Most are excited to hear that my childhood was quite ordinary; a stereotypical, middle class, 1970s North American childhood. I lived in the suburbs, ate Campbell's mushroom soup and drank Cherry Coke. I loved *The Brady Bunch, Bewitched, Match Game* and Saturday morning cartoons. If there was anything unusual about me, it was my need for constant motion. I ran, skipped, jumped, cart wheeled and did back handsprings endlessly, indoors and out, winter and summer, incessantly talking all the while.

Outwardly, my childhood was very normal, except maybe for an early fascination with bones, the result of breaking my ankle several times; a fascination that probably lead me to anthropology, and an unusual interest in dead people. I did grow up in a tricky home with an emotionally volatile and extremely unpredictable parent. I recall, from a young age, constantly having to project myself home before walking through the front door to get a feel for what I was about to walk into – a survival skill that served me well, and I'm sure contributed to my telepathic abilities later in life.

My answer to the question "Are you born telepathic, or can you learn?", however, is "Yes", and "Yes". Like many questions about consciousness and telepathy, the answer is far more complicated than the question presupposes. I think we are *all* born telepathic, very telepathic, but quickly learn to hide or suppress our natural abilities, unless we are encouraged to use them, or forced to. The process happens slowly throughout childhood, the result of many little moments where we discover that grownups don't understand our telepathic experience of the world, and that these experiences scare them.

As a child, you may remember walking into a room and feeling or simply knowing that something was off. After inquiring you might have been told "Everything's fine, sweetie" and maybe given a worried or stern look. Well-meaning parents, myself included, in an effort to protect our children from grownup problems, sometimes pretend that everything is fine when it isn't, leaving kids confused about their psychic senses until they eventually learn to disregard them altogether. In many families, children's intuitively bang-on questions, however innocently asked, can result in a hard and fast lesson in ignoring telepathic cues: children's intuitions all too often hit on family secrets, or shameful, emotionally charged issues that grownups know not to talk about.

The discomfort, alarm or outright fear that many adults react with when children talk about very ordinary psychic experiences is also a clear and unequivocal lesson for children. For example, my friend's niece once announced to him, while being pushed on a playground swing, that she could see pretty colors around people. My friend was dumbfounded, and didn't know how to respond. Although he was deeply interested, he was so shocked he couldn't muster a response. He continued to push her on the swing in silence, a response I'm sure his niece felt and noted. Silence speaks volumes, but sometimes adults react to such information with much more than silence.

Another friend of the family once explained to me that while grocery shopping with her young son, he stopped to listen to an Asian couple carrying on a conversation in another language and announced, "Mommy, I understand what they're saying." She pulled her son away from the couple in alarm and dragged him out of the store, leaving her groceries behind. I startled her again when I pointed out that it wasn't surprising that her son had taken taekwondo (a Korean martial art) throughout his youth and had grown up to marry a Korean girl.

The best answer then, to the question of "Are we born telepathic? Or can we learn?" is that we are all born telepathic, very telepathic, and have never stopped being telepathic. We have simply learned to ignore and explain away the telepathic experiences we are all having, all the time. We are immersed in telepathic experiences every moment of our lives, and deeply influenced by our telepathic environments – unconsciously – largely because of our cultural refusal to acknowledge the reality and value of the telepathic part of ourselves in conscious and upfront ways.

Learning to be telepathic, or better said, remembering your natural telepathy, is simply about bringing consciousness to something that is and has been happening outside of your conscious awareness all the time, your entire life. Sit down, be still, and watch for signs, Native American wisdom tells us. In stillness, under the chatter of our thinking minds, we find our connection to all that is, and our authentic selves. When we bring consciousness to this profoundly intelligent part of ourselves, we can become truly conscious beings who understand ourselves, our unique contributions to the greater whole, and the consequences of our thoughts and actions.

As far as my childhood telepathic experiences go, like most people, I'm sure I have forgotten more than I can recall. I do remember hearing a voice in my head one night as a young child while looking for a snack in the kitchen. The voice was clearly male, but said exactly what I was about to say, just before I would say it. When I mentioned the voice to my parents I saw the look of horror on their faces. That was the moment I shut down my clairaudience, or psychic hearing, a psychic sense that hasn't returned since for me.

I also remember sitting on the curb when I was eight,

wondering where my future husband was. What followed was like a daydream mixed with a knowing that contained more novelty and detail than I thought my imagination capable of. I had a very clear knowing that he wasn't in Canada; that we were separated by water; that he would eventually move to Canada, and that his name started with R and had three letters. My husband, Rod, was living in Jamaica when I was eight. He returned to Canada after living another decade overseas, and our lives synchronistically intertwined a few years later.

When I was 15, I remember dreaming about my boyfriend breaking up with me under a street light on a dark night in the rain. The dream was so vivid, when I woke up, I remembered it as if it had just happened. A week later, my boyfriend broke up with me, at night, in the rain, on the street corner from my dream. My dumbfounded reaction wasn't about the breakup. I was so shocked by the perfect unfoldment of my dream, I barely registered the hurt about the breakup itself.

The most dramatic telepathic experience of my life marked the end of my childhood, more than it was part of it. For years I hid the details from everyone including my friends and family out of fear, and because of the crippling anxiety the incident left me with. I was twelve at the time, sitting with two friends, halfway up the grassy slope of a man made hill about thirty feet high. The hill was nestled between several sports fields and a patch of forest, perfect for tobogganing in the winter or rolling down in the summer. We were playing a game we had played all summer, a game we called trance. We would take turns lying down on our backs and massaging light circles on each other's temples while we counted down from a hundred. Sometimes we would do little guided meditations, talking to each other about walking through clouds or fields, or whatever came to us. Thinking back, I have no idea where we got the idea, we were simply being kids, playing.

Trance got boring after a while, and we settled in on the grassy slope to stare at the sky and talk. Sitting in the grass, I remember suddenly feeling uncomfortable, like I needed to get up and move. As I noticed the feeling, I heard a soft female voice in my head say, "You have to move, a motorcycle is coming." I didn't think. I got up and walked down the little slope, into the nearby trees. Being in the trees eased my stress and the sense of urgency I had been struck with sitting on the slope. I could hear an engine in the distance, but the fields around the hill were constantly being mowed, so the engine sound was not out of the ordinary.

From the trees, I caught the flash of a motorcycle flying through the air in my periphery. A young man had decided to cut through the schoolyard on his dirt bike and jump the hill, without checking his landing zone, where my friends still sat. I looked over to see the motorcycle sliding to a stop with one of my friends underneath. I ran over to her, but knew immediately that she was gone, although I didn't get the call confirming her death until around ten o'clock that night. I turned to find that my other friend had been hit too, and was face down, unconscious, higher up the slope. Suddenly, I realized I was there alone with the man who had just killed my friend.

I ran to a nearby community pool and called 911, then I had to call my friends' parents. I can still hear the heartbreak in their mothers' voices. I know that sometime after I made the phone calls, before the ambulance came, I ran back to my friends, and the guy who had just run them both over. He did his best to calm me down. I think I was in shock. I remember being wrapped in a red blanket and having to give my statement in the back of a police car. I was petrified, and sure that if I had told the police or anyone else about playing trance, or about the voice in my head, that I would be blamed for the tragedy. I had known a motorcycle was coming, not consciously enough to have saved my friends, but I couldn't get beyond my own survivor guilt to understand that myself at the time, let alone have explained it to anyone. I told the police everything I remembered, but not the whole truth, not about playing trance or the voice in my head that told me to move.

I walked home alone, pushing two bikes, my own and my dead friend's. When I got home, I realized that I was home alone, or might as well have been. My parents were in Florida, and my babysitter, ill-equipped to handle such a situation, didn't know what to say. Not that she could have said or done anything to make my nightmare disappear. So I sat on my bed, sad, cold, and traumatized, feeling completely alone. In the quiet, I remember a feeling slowly coming over me, subtly telling me that everything was going to be okay. I remember feeling like I was connected to something or someone I couldn't see. It felt like religion, or what religion was supposed to feel like; like the connection was real and strong even though I couldn't see it or hear it. I just knew it. And that was really my introduction to telepathy. A rude slap of an introduction, but an introduction nonetheless.

My fears around sharing the whole truth about what happened on the day of the accident turned out to be well-founded. The man who killed my friend, and put my other friend in a coma for months, followed by years of physical and brain injury rehab, was put on trial for criminal negligence. I was called as a witness, and cross-examined with an argumentative, accusatory zeal that I'm astonished at even today when I go back and read the court transcripts. I remembered the man on the motorcycle saying, "God damn it, I knew this would happen," as he got up from the crash. I told the police so in my statement right after the accident. My recollection might have been the projected guilt of a traumatized 12 year old, but I really think that this man realized right after the accident that a part of him, the part of himself that we have all been taught to ignore, did know the accident was going to happen before it happened, just like I did.

The defense lawyer grilled me to tears over my police statement in front of the court, insinuating that I had lied, that I might be in trouble for doing so, and insisting that I must have been mistaken, because his client had gone to bible college to study to become a minister, and therefore couldn't have said such a thing as he was obviously a good person. For a few minutes, I was put on trial more than the motorcyclist, who I now realize was just a kid too, at 19. I can't imagine the abuse I would have suffered from this lawyer, and the medical professionals that he undoubtedly would have arranged to discredit my recollection, had I told the police about my entire experience and the voice I heard. I imagine the subsequent social ostracism, and the medical treatment to cure me of hearing voices would have been far worse. The outcome of the trial was a $500 fine for trespassing for the motorcyclist and a lifelong distrust of the justice system and organized religion for me.

Today, looking back, I now think that by playing trance just before the accident, I had inadvertently slipped into an altered state of consciousness and a part of me knew what was going to happen before it happened – not consciously or clearly enough to warn my friends – but just enough to feel discomfort and unconsciously save myself. It could have been an angel, a spirit guide, or another being of higher power, whispering in my ear I suppose, and many people will say with certainty that it must have been. However, I don't recall sensing the presence of another being. I distinctly recall the voice sounding like my own, but older, and I haven't really worked with spirit guides or angels since; not to say that such beings don't exist, or that I haven't had some powerful experiences with beings that fit the description. I just think that overly focusing on such beings can be disempowering, distracting us from understanding and developing our own natural abilities.

After working in altered states for years, I can say with a fair degree of certainty that when I was inspired to move because a motorcycle was coming that day, I wasn't doing anything special, and I wasn't 'saved' by angels or guides. Part of my mind was simply doing what all of our minds do, all the time: collecting and integrating telepathic information about our environment, and the future. I just happened to be in a state of heightened receptivity, and fidgety enough to need to move in response to the information I felt; information that I regretfully didn't share because of its subtle nature.

The accident was an incredibly hard lesson in learning to pay attention to and trust my inner experiences, even when they seemed random, strange or crazy. It was a lesson that took years of therapy to unpack and forgive myself for learning at such a cost. It is a lesson that served me well in my career as a psychic medium and telepath though, and one that would serve many people well: trust yourself and others' genuine inner experiences. Our inner experiences are not random or strange, they inform us about our environment, the people we are connected to and the future. Learning to understand and use our inner experiences to guide our actions and decisions, and teaching our children to do so, has the potential to save many lives, and that's just the beginning.

It was 10 years after the accident before I felt safe enough in the world again to get back in touch with the telepathic part of myself, and to trust that nothing bad was going to happen if I did. It happened rather inadvertently, the result of years of listening to various guided meditations to try and calm the anxiety I was riddled with for years after the accident, and as a result of reading Robert Monroe's book *Journeys Out of the Body*. One day during meditation, after following Monroe's instructions, I rolled out of my physical frame and looked back at my deeply relaxed body in my bed. To tell you the truth, it was a success that scared me, but it also shifted my perspective on life. Before the experience of looking back at my body, I had identified my body as myself, a machine that was me. Like a car, or any other machine, I would eventually break down and die, if I didn't manage to wreck myself first. Suddenly, I was viscerally aware that I wasn't my body; I wasn't the vehicle, I was the driver, the 'ghost in the machine'. I knew then that I would walk away from my body when it eventually broke down, from age or accident. I would be okay. I would still exist, and I would still be me; I just wouldn't have my bodily vehicle anymore.

The relief of knowing that death wasn't the end should have been profound, and it was a turning point in my life, but part of me just couldn't accept that I would survive death, no matter how real my experiences had been. Part of me continued to doubt, analyze, judge and question the reality of my out of body experiences in a misguided effort to keep me safe through stress, worry and fear. My analytical mind wasn't willing to trust the 'spiritual' part of my being, let alone relinquish control of my life to it. As a result, I didn't experiment with out of body journeys very much, or venture very far. I did get good enough at relaxing my body into a state of sleep, while still staying conscious, that I could do so almost at will, even if I didn't leave my body. It was mostly a matter of making the conscious decision to do it, realizing that I could do it, and letting go of my analytical mind's fears and doubts about the process. Once you set the intention to have an out of body experience, that's half the battle. It wasn't until I watched an episode of the television show *Crossing Over* that I discovered I could do anything useful or objectively validatable in an altered state of consciousness though.

John Edward, one of the best-known psychic-mediums in the world, had a television show that first aired in 1999 called *Crossing Over*. The show consisted almost entirely of John performing mediumship readings in front of groups, then having the people who received readings explain how the information John provided fit their lives and the lives of their dead people. By this time, I had graduated university with a degree in anthropology and a second in visual arts. After years of academic training in an environment where only what you could measure was considered real, I honestly believed at first that *Crossing Over* was a staged 'reality' show, with paid actors, or that audience members were being paid to keep quiet that they were acting. Like a good anthropologist though, I watched and observed, looking for patterns, motivations and holes in people's stories, assessing audience members' authenticity and gullibility the whole time. I was fascinated, and the more I watched, the harder it became for me to convince myself that everybody on the show was lying, or that there were that many good actors willing to participate in such a show. When John explained during one episode that you don't need a medium to communicate with dead people, that you can do it yourself, I decided to give it a try.

It happened to be the day of my brother's birthday, just a few hours before I was to be at my parents' house for dinner to celebrate. I sat down and closed my eyes thinking I'd just stare at the inside of my eyelids and see if I could see anything. I strained with my eyes to find images until I found a happy medium between effort and ease and settled into my vision. I held it softly. Suddenly, like an image on a developing photograph, I saw a house. Then, five minutes or so later, I softly watched more pictures appear on the back of my eyelids, pictures that looked like moving photo negatives.

The first image I saw was of my grandparents' house. I hadn't seen it since I was eight years old. It was light blue in my mind's eye, which I thought was odd, since I recalled the house being white. The image zoomed in, around to the backyard where I could see a clothesline, as if I was being given a tour. Suddenly, I was in the house, looking at a corner cabinet that held my grandmother's china. Then, suddenly, I was standing in the desert watching an RV drive by. I knew somehow that it was going from California to Arizona, and it was my grandfather's trip. Like the blue house, the RV didn't make any sense. I'd heard that my grandfather had never travelled outside of Southwestern Ontario his entire life. Then, I felt like I WAS my grandfather, standing behind my brother at around age 12, with my hands on his shoulders while he sat on the bench between shifts playing hockey. Again, the image didn't make any sense to me because my grandfather had died before my brother was born. Then, I felt like I was supposed to say, "I'm with Harold."

A few hours later, at my parents' house, I checked out the details I had seen earlier. I pulled my mother aside and asked about the blue house, the RV trip and the patterns I'd seen on the china. To my amazement, every detail checked out. She confirmed all of it. My grandparents' house had been blue before I was born, my grandfather had taken one trip in his life, in an RV trip from California to Arizona, and my mother told me that the china patterns I drew her matched her mother's exactly. Harold, I learned, had been my grandfather's best man and best friend. My mother knew exactly what the image of him standing with my brother between hockey shifts meant.

My grandfather died of a heart attack while shoveling snow. He was clearing his driveway before coming to visit for my eighth birthday. My mother was planning to surprise him with the news that he was going to have another grandchild. She never got to tell him about my brother, and had always regretted waiting to tell him in person. The message in the image of my grandfather with his hands on my brother's shoulders, watching my brother grow up playing hockey, something my grandfather would have loved, along with the other validations, couldn't have been clearer: he did know about my brother, he hadn't missed watching him grow up, and there was nothing for my mother to regret. It was her gift on my brother's birthday.

Needless to say, my interest was piqued. I lay down to stare at the inside of my eyelids almost every day after that, waiting and watching images appear. I would find a friend, family member or friend of the family that was open to hearing anything I might pick up, and I would lie down, close my eyes and wait for the images to begin. I would write down what I saw and then call the person to explain the images I saw. Pretty soon, I had run out of friends and family to test my new skills out on, and I started reading friends of friends, then my brother's frat buddies, then their sorority girlfriends. Somewhere along the line people started calling me for readings.

My brother was serendipitously enrolled in a psychology class at the time at the University of Western Ontario called *Altered States of Consciousness,* taught by professor Imants Baruss. Survival of consciousness after death, along with mediumship, happened to be on the syllabus. Months after I'd started experimenting with mediumship and documenting the experiences I was having, I ended up back at Western, where I'd graduated a few years before, in Imants' office, two of my journals in hand. I'd ended up in the right place.

Professor Imants Baruss has now been studying and teaching about human consciousness for over thirty years and is the author of numerous books and scientific papers on the subject. He is one of only a handful of academics in the world currently studying consciousness, and is one of the world's top experts on the subject. Imants not only helped me understand my abilities, he invited me to demonstrate them in a few of his classes, so his students would get to see and experience firsthand what they were studying. I ended up spending the next 12 years visiting Imants' classes as a guest speaker, to read a few students, and then have the class analyze and try to explain what they saw and experienced. I learned a lot from all the questions students asked over the years, and our attempts to answer their questions. Over the years, my abilities improved, my understanding of what I think is a basic human ability got clearer and clearer, and I learned to apply the ability in new ways.

I couldn't have imagined for most of my life that all the things I can now do with telepathic abilities were possible at all, let alone possible for me, including the ability to:

- communicate with dead people
- communicate with animals, both living and dead

- psychically perceive living people's thoughts, beliefs and emotions (with caveats I'll explain later), and how they have and will play out in repeating life patterns
- obtain certain types of information about anything or anyone, past, present or future (information that is often validatable, which I could not have had prior knowledge of, researched or guessed)
- preview possible and probable futures, get a sense of the likelihood of them coming to pass, and the steps people can take to make desired possible futures happen
- work with people to fine-tune and align their visions of themselves, and the future, to co-create relationships and experiences with other conscious people with an ease, genius and power beyond anything a logical mind could ever conceive or orchestrate
- understand things, and other beings, on a level beyond anything language could possibly convey

All I really needed to develop these abilities was permission. Permission to believe in myself and the fact that my strange, random and crazy thoughts, along with the images and feelings I could perceive when I meditated with intention, were not strange, random or crazy at all. I would like to give others the same permission, and share a few of the things I've learned over the years about telepathic abilities, our essential telepathic nature, and what it means to be telepathically connected to the wider world.

Leaving the Dark Ages

Any sufficiently advanced technology is indistinguishable from magic.

When a distinguished but elderly scientist states that something is impossible,

he is very probably wrong.

The only way of discovering the limits of the possible is to venture a little way past them into the impossible.

~ Arthur C. Clarke's Laws of Prediction

For the first 15 years of my career, I referred to myself as a psychic-medium, purely out of forced practicality. The term never really captured the fullness of the work I did and, given the choice, I would much rather have avoided all the baggage that came with the label. Most people have let go of thinking of fortune-telling, curses, séances, woo-woo moments, ghosts and spirits when the term psychic-medium comes up, but stereotypes and irrational fears endure. People still tend to freak out when they find out what I do for a living, sometimes in fear, sometimes in arrogant disbelief. I spend a lot of time dispelling myths and calming irrational fears about being psychic; time that I think could be better spent talking about what we can do with psychic abilities, or actually doing something useful with them.

I now introduce myself as a *conscious living coach*, the best term I can come up with to explain what I actually do with my psychic abilities: help people to bring consciousness to every area of their lives to solve problems and live happier, more enjoyable and accomplished lives. I also prefer the term *telepath* over psychic-medium. Telepathy is simply defined as mind to mind, or consciousness to consciousness communication. Mediumship is a form of telepathy, along with intuition, clairvoyance, animal communication, remote viewing, remote healing, and a range of other psychic abilities and phenomena. It's all the same ability, applied in slightly different ways.

I think of telepathy as a skill with broad applications rather than a mystical ability to turn to in secret, when everything else has failed. Used openly with skill and purpose, telepathy is a technology that can be applied to every area of human endeavor with tremendous individual and collective benefits. Contrary to popular desire, psychic abilities and telepathy don't work well for picking lottery numbers or winning horses. Telepathy isn't consistently useful when competition for personal gain at the expense of others is the aim. Predicting the future to avoid negative and unintended consequences does work well, but the true power and potential of telepathy lies in co-creating the future, not predicting it. Telepathy is far better suited, and exponentially more powerful, when it is used openly, to facilitate cooperation and creativity. The real promise and power of telepathy is in its astounding ability to orchestrate and facilitate all sorts of cooperative relationships, interactions, adaptations and transformations.

To appreciate the sophistication and genius telepathy offers in this regard, we have to look to the miracle of nature. If you look closely, you will notice that everything in nature from schooling fish, to migrating birds, to spawning salmon, to pollinating bees, to the cells in our bodies, functions through a sort of telepathic connection. Anyone who has spent time in nature, or studied it scientifically, is left with a sense of appreciation for the astounding intelligence that appears to orchestrate the natural world. Nature knows when it's time: when it is time to grow, to hibernate, to migrate, to reproduce, and when it's time to die. Trees know when and how to grow, how to harvest sunlight and how to work with bacteria to get nutrients from the soil. Your body knows how to move, grow, breathe and work with bacteria in your gut to digest food. Animals know where to travel to find food, or dig dens, even in a changing world, sometimes as if they know the future: digging dens high on riverbanks to avoid once in a decade spring floods or collectively seeking shelter hours before severe weather or earthquakes.

This knowing, instinctual and collective intelligence we see throughout the natural world cannot be found or fully explained by the DNA, brain function or the intelligence of individual organisms. There is something more going on, something bigger, something that looks a lot like a vast collective intelligence coordinating and orchestrating the miracle of nature, the beautiful and immeasurably complex dance of symbiotic, competitive, and synergistic relationships we see at every level of the natural world. Though we can often glimpse this intelligence at work, we can't explain how it works through physical-material means. The deep interconnectedness we see everywhere in nature functions through an invisible connection that can't be sampled, measured or seen under a microscope. The connection is nonphysical: a sort of telepathic connection.

Telepathy is universal to all nature, as well as the human experience. I now teach the concept of natural telepathy rather than law of attraction, karma or destiny because at the heart of all of these concepts is a universal and natural telepathic connection. When we tune into and consciously use our own natural telepathy, we can tap into the same extraordinary collective intelligence that orchestrates the miracle of nature to guide and inspire our own lives. In doing so, we can create wildly fulfilling, joyful and abundant lives for ourselves, to the benefit of one another and the rest of the planet: a perspective I like to refer to as win-win-win, or collective synergy.

If we can get over our collective fear and embrace what is a natural human ability and, really, our first language, telepathy might even help us accomplish results on a global level that few of us can even dream of now, without negative and unintended consequences that harm others and the planet. As with other soft technologies such as language, the telephone, or the Internet, the promise and power of telepathy as a technology will only be realized when many people begin using it consciously and cooperatively. Few people dreamt of, let alone predicted, the far-reaching ways that the Internet and wireless technologies have transformed lives around the globe. The next wave of revolutionary technology might have less to do with little black boxes and more to do with how we collectively use and navigate our own consciousness.

Sadly, even though the reality of telepathy is a broadly proven scientific fact of public record,[1] many people still can't get past their own skepticism and the question of whether psychic abilities are real or not. It's natural to be skeptical, but more natural, I think, to be curious, and to follow your curiosity. Those who do embrace the reality of these abilities often can't get past the awe or amazement that these abilities arouse when experienced firsthand, are stuck in wonder and proving the existence of these abilities, and don't do anything productive with these abilities. Collectively, we can't even get to the interesting questions, like, "What can we do with telepathy?" or "How much could telepathy improve our lives and collective fate?"

I've done my best in recent years to distance myself from any talk of spirits, ghosts or the paranormal, as well as the words such as 'psychic-medium', because the fear these words arouse distracts from the real magic and benefits of telepathy. That said, I still spend a lot of time talking to dead people (I prefer the term dead people to spirit or disincarnate – it's less spooky – dead people are just people, without physical bodies). I've learned a lot talking to dead people over the years, and I think the key to understanding how consciousness functions happens to lie in the answer to a question people ask a lot: "What's it like to be dead?". So even though this is a book about consciousness and telepathy, "What's it like to be dead?" is where we have to start.

Although the question comes up a lot, people tend to avoid the real question, and the real answer, by asking something like:

"What's it like on the other side?" as if death is a vacation destination. Death is an uncomfortable subject that people tend to avoid, to their detriment. When we get comfortable with the question of death, a huge range of fears and anxieties often disappear from our lives. It's a very important question, and I spent years taking every opportunity I could to ask dead people the question directly. For a long time, the bizarre range of seemingly evasive stories I received made it seem as if the question was not an important one. In fact, most dead people I asked the question of didn't answer at all, as if nothing *was* the answer.

Of course, talking to dead people isn't like having an ordinary conversation. They communicate without words. They show me images and share perspectives and feelings with me. If you've ever played charades or Pictionary, you can imagine some of the challenges of my job. I have had lots of dead people show me pictures that might be construed as something like heaven. A three year old who died after being struck by a car once showed me that, when he wasn't visiting his living siblings in the playroom of their new home, he went to school. The school he showed me was outside in the grass, which was blue, and there were lots of bunnies hopping around. There were other kids there, and he liked his teacher a lot. More than a few men I've talked to have shown me images of themselves fishing, or golfing 'on the other side' in stunning landscapes, but for the most part, dead people don't share a lot of specific information on the subject.

Communication challenges aside, I realize in hindsight that the stories dead people show me aren't evasive at all, rather the stories *are* the answer, but not the kind of answer we're used to. You have to put a lot of stories and pieces together to get the kind of answer living people want. Dead people don't give the types of answer we're used to, I think, because their minds simply don't work the way our earthly thinking minds do. Many of the things that we are so deathly concerned with while alive don't even register as something to think or talk about when you're dead. Rather than what it's like on the other side, or what they do when they're not talking to me, most of the dead people I talk to simply want to connect with their loved ones, let them know that they're alright, reminisce and maybe help them heal something so they can make their time here on earth their highest quality experience. In fact, the first thing all dead people almost universally share with their loved ones is "I'm good" by sharing images of themselves smiling, youthful, vital, strong, healthy and happy, which is probably really the best indication of what it's like to be dead.

Dead people also love to talk about what they loved in life, and it's even easier for them to communicate about an interest if it's also an interest of mine. If I share an interest with a dead person, we share a vocabulary, both sensory and verbal, and the passion and emotions they share with me are heightened, which can make for some entertaining exchanges. For example, I love to cook, which means that anyone who comes through who also loved to cook in life can, and will, show me foods they used to make, how they made them, and sometimes the ingredients. Sometimes they share who's making a favorite dish now, which ingredients are being left out, what new ingredients are being added, and sometimes even all the ways the recipe has since been mangled by the new cooks, all so I can rib living family members. Maybe it's partly because I love to cook so much, or possibly just that food is what brings family together most often, but I spend a lot of time talking food with dead people.

Sometimes dead people share what they've learned since their death. They often come through with a completely clean, objective retelling of the facts of their life, often taking full responsibility for their life, and for some, even owning up to things they would never have owned up to in life. I once even had the very strange experience of having a conversation with a dead mobster who had killed a lot of people. It was already happening before we realized who he was. I didn't feel any danger or any kind of threat. He wasn't evil or unpleasant, he just shared the facts of his life. That was all. No muss, no fuss.

What I want to make really clear is that the dead people I talk to are still people with fully intact personalities, preferences, likes, dislikes, memories and some, though not all, emotions. They're very much like normal people to talk to, except they communicate through thoughts that mimic sensory information rather than words, and are never in a bad mood (with two notable though rare exceptions). Their personalities, quirks and habits come through loud and clear. The less I get in the way, the clearer the personality of whomever I'm talking to comes through. Dead people reference and communicate with the same quirks, mannerisms, memories and preferences they had in life. The only thing they have left behind, other than their body, seems to be the part of their mind that created stress, anger, worry, hate and fear while they were on earth. Turns out we have a lot to learn from the dead.

I do need to take a moment to talk about the two exceptions to the universal beneficence of dead people. Most dead people report experiencing death as an instant relief from physical and emotional pain, as well as from negative or impaired thinking. Alzheimer's patients report their minds functioning perfectly upon death, and having spent protracted periods outside of their bodies during the latter stages of their disease. People who have died of cancer and other such progressive illnesses also report popping in and out of their bodies as they transitioned towards physical death, especially when heavily medicated or in pain. Car crash victims who passed instantly often show images of the crash scene from inside the car and then from about ten feet above looking down. Sometimes they imply a popping sensation before they tell me "… and then I was out… it wasn't that bad."

I've never met a murder victim who had any interest in

helping police catch their killer, let alone seeking justice or vengeance. Every murder victim I've met has encouraged their family and friends to focus on their life, on good times together and on connection, not on a brief moment of tragedy. From their perspective, they can see and understand how everything works itself out, seeing justice and karma from a much higher perspective than we do. Even the most innocent victims of heinous crimes, like a young local girl, who was abducted and murdered by someone she knew, who I've talked to a number of times, doesn't want to talk about her killer. Murder victims want to visit and enjoy their time and connection with the people they loved in life, and often encourage living family members to let go of anger and the desire to catch or punish their killers.

A few dead people, however, do seem to need some time to let go of their earthly minds' thinking patterns. For example, a distant neighbor of mine's father once showed up in my driveway as I was leaving my house. He was panic-stricken and distraught. He had been murdered only hours before, just a few kilometers from my home, and was so deep in his feelings of panic and fear about the fight he was just in, that his focus kept him attached to his physical life. As I talked to him though, helping him notice that he was okay, even though he didn't have a physical body anymore, his state shifted. He became less demanding and fearful, and softened both emotionally and energetically. It only took a few minutes for him to calm down and go on his way. Quite a few people seem to need a few days, usually the time between their death and their funeral, to acclimate to their new state, and many still behave as if they have a physical body during that time, getting around by riding in cars, buses, or by walking for example.

I have also had the experience of speaking with dead people who were addicts or narcissists in life, deeply focused in anger and drama, whose negative focus continued for a short time after their deaths. I have done follow-up sessions with a few of these people over the course of several years following their deaths and I've noticed that, in every case, these people become more and more accountable, apologetic, wise and lovely as time passes, allowing their living families to reconcile, forgive and come to terms with how they were in life, as well as see how far they've come after their deaths.

I cringe to bring up the second exception to the universal beneficence of dead people because of the stigma and fear associated with it. Still, I must responsibly address the entities I call the loveless: the negative dead people who won't, or can't, let go of their earthly focus and accompanying negative emotions, sometimes referred to as earthbound spirits. Such people, who do not seem to have any loving connections, or perhaps the capacity to love, can show up while working in altered states, particularly when there's a negative focus like investigating murders, or paranormal phenomena.

Most haunting-type phenomena I have investigated (back when I was interested) have not involved dead people at all. Most haunting phenomena in my experience stem from energy signatures, sort of like memories having been imprinted upon spaces; memories that play over and over in loops that people entering the space can experience. There is really no danger from such energy signatures, unless you consistently focus on the energy signature, and start to unconsciously play it out in your life. However, focusing on anything negative or unpleasant in altered states, doing such work with a fearful mindset, or in secret as if it's something to be ashamed of, can bring resonant negative beings, or things into your awareness. Avoiding such experiences requires clear and purely positive intentions before doing any altered state work, a positive emotional state, and preferably wise and experienced guidance. Even with disciplined focus and thorough preparation though, unwanted and unpleasant interactions can and do happen at first.

If negative encounters do happen, in my experience, if you

believe you are safe and act accordingly, you are safe. You have a body, and anyone that doesn't can't physically harm you; however, they can impact your energetic body, scare, and annoy you if you let them. Calm confidence, knowing that you are safe, along with learning to firmly shift your focus away from unpleasant things and exerting firm and healthy boundaries in every regard is the best psychic protection in altered states, and in life, that I've been able to find so far. I am not alone in having had some tough experiences though, such as being shown grizzly images or being aggressively screamed at while I'm trying to concentrate. This happens with some regularity in the general population but rarely gets spoken of, to the detriment of many.

Statistically, around one in ten people have heard voices spontaneously and many of these people end up dealing with such experiences in fear and isolation, fearing that, if they seek help, they will be met with one of two answers, if not both: they're imagining things, or they're crazy. These encounters with the loveless can be emotionally scarring or traumatizing if you let them, but they don't need to be. I think we need to acknowledge that these encounters do occur, and collectively learn how to deal with them in clear, effective, and empowered ways. You don't need to fear the entire universe because of one bad neighborhood and a few miserable people. What I would like to stress is that the potential applications of telepathy are endless, and do not need to involve the paranormal, solving crimes, dead people, or anything negative or unpleasant at all.

Apart from the anomalies above, what is universally consistent about the dead people I talk to is their absence of anger, guilt, stress and worry. They come through to me with peace and ease. They don't communicate anything to me from a place of fear or stress. It's as if they are missing the ability to feel negative emotions altogether. They will often share the kinds of emotions they lived with in their life but only to explain their circumstances or perspective. They never do blame, or become angry in the moment, ever. Some dead people even apologize for their negative emotions in life, but they never communicate from a place of guilt or shame. It's not like they've lost any personality; quiet people are still quiet; people who were loud or obnoxious in life are still just as loud, and usually the first to come through, sometimes even interjecting over other dead people long after they've supposedly finished talking. What dead people share with me most of all is love, sometimes with such overwhelming intensity that it makes me cry. I feel deeply lucky to be able to communicate this way; it's a profoundly sacred and beautiful experience.

Although it may seem trite, I cannot emphasize enough that while working in altered states the most important element or ingredient to include is unconditional love. Think of love as a way of focusing the mind, a powerful skill and ability, and a measure and flavor of connection. The ability to attain, retain and focus from a loving state is, I believe, what permits telepathic communication, as well as what keeps you safe in altered states. You can end up in some unpleasant places if your focus slips towards fear, anger, anxiety or judgement in altered states of consciousness. Emotions in altered states are like Velcro hurled out into the dark in search of a match: there are plenty of matches to any emotional state and you get back what you put out.

Unconditionally loving states, states of pure love, harmlessness and gentle curiosity are required to create the telepathic connections that allow conscious telepathic communication. I don't think it's a coincidence that avatars, sages and saints, people who have historically been reported to have various superpowers, from knowing the future and the nature of the universe to making wine out of water, have all also been living embodiments of love and have primarily taught about love. Unfortunately, I think the institutionalization of these teachings about love has created widespread confusion between concepts of what love can look like, and the state of being that such concepts point to and flow from.

Untangling some of this confusion, the notion that love has conditions, is about being nice, grandiose gestures, romance, sex or self-sacrifice, is a key step in accessing and understanding telepathic abilities. To untangle such confusion, I often refer my clients to heart-centered therapy, or suggest reading material like Diane Zimberoff's book *Breaking Free from the Victim Trap*, or *The Power of TED** by David Emerald. Diane and David both eloquently describe the life dramas that ensue when we place conditions on love and acceptance, and live on the co-dependent triangle: in the roles of victim, persecutor and rescuer, roles Zimberoff says seven out of ten families relate to one another and function through. To get a sense of your own ability to access loving states and telepathic connection, consider the places and ways you already love, feel loved and experience joy in your life. These are the places and ways you are already in connection in life, and are excellent places to begin exploring from.

When you start putting all the pieces together, dead people's complete absence of stress and fear makes sense: they're dead; they don't have to worry about survival because their death has already happened. From what I can deduce after years of what seemed like cute stories and cryptic babbling, dead people seem to spend time creating whatever experience they want in a shared, spontaneously created environment with the ease and speed of thought. Think about that for a second. You can think of your favorite food and your favorite place, and your favorite thing to do, and boom, you're eating your favorite food, in your favorite place, doing your favorite thing instantaneously as you think the thought. No waiting, no compromise, no working for weeks or months to save up for what you want, no planning, scheming, competing or worrying about variables or surprises.

While you entertain yourself with your favorite things, others can join you, or not, and when you're over it, you can go play in someone else's creation or a new one of your own. Heaven is a good name for a place like that if you ask me. I have never once had a dead person reference lack, pain or judgement in their experience since their passing in any way, let alone the existence of hell, no matter how they were in life, including the hundreds of people I've talked to who have taken their own lives. Now, I haven't gone looking for such places either, and they may exist in some way, but no dead person has ever taken me there, nor do I have any interest in seeing or experiencing such places, if they do exist at all.

So, the first part of the answer to the question "What's it like to be dead?" is – it's liberating. The problems of earth are gone and there don't seem to be any new problems let alone any judgement, fire or brimstone. There is no hunger, no vulnerable body to fuel or protect from disease or attack, no money to earn, no rent to pay, no ageing and no need to argue over anything. There's never a rush because there isn't the same time crunch we have the minute we are born into a body with an expiry date. The environment dead people seem to exist in is so different from the environment we live in, that dead people have no need for the part of our minds that we use to function and survive on this planet: the part of our minds that I call the *survivor mind* or the *bio-mind*. Without their earthly survivor minds, dead people's minds are much cleaner, faster, freer and more objective than our thinking minds; clear facts and insight minus the running emotional commentary that so often bogs down our daily lives. For me, the difference between dead people's minds and most living people's minds is jarring and clear, with a few notable exceptions.

Some living people's minds are very much like dead people's minds. The minds of more than a few exceptional and lovely people on this planet aren't bogged down with the emotional baggage, worries, guilt, anger and stress that most of us carry around. Almost every living person has moments in life where they escape their survivor mind, drop their worries, judgements and fears, show up in the moment, and suddenly turn into lovely, radiant beings, just like our dead friends. These moments are also often moments of clarity, wisdom, love and connection, or moments of epiphany where brilliant ideas show up, amazing things are accomplished and beautiful things happen. These are the moments and times when we lose ourselves in something we love, and time flies by; times of connection, delight, laughter, fun and joy.

What I've come to realize is that although we all have survivor minds, and we need them to function on the planet, we also have what I call connected minds: the part of our minds that dead people live in, that we all come from, and will all return to. You could call this part of yourself your spirit or soul, but I don't think such words capture the true nature of this part of the self. A soul is something you have, protect and save, not something that is part of you, that you can access at will, just as you can access your thinking mind. Spirits can seem scary rather than something that is an intimate part of you, a part of you that is more You than your body and thoughts are You; and our spirits are certainly not generally thought of as the true source of inspiration, clarity, creativity, love and peace within ourselves.

We all have connected minds, and our connected minds are more who we are than our thinking survivor minds: our connected minds are our authentic selves. We all naturally cycle between our connected minds and our survivor minds organically all day, but we can choose which part of our minds we want to spend time in and use. Most of us have become so focused in our survivor minds and bogged down with earthly problems and worries that we spend little time in our connected minds. We have forgotten that we can go into our connected minds at will, and we've forgotten how to get there. Many of us have tuned right out of our connection to the greater whole altogether, and can no longer get in touch with the part of ourselves from which inspiration, happiness, and ease flows. We spend little time in connection, and live mostly in our problem solving, worrying, stressed-out survivor minds, so much so that we have come to fear our natural telepathic connection to the world.

To get back in touch with this sacred part of ourselves, our connected minds, and remember how to access their power and potential, we need to go back to the second part of the answer to the question of "What's it like to be dead?". The answer: it's not that different from being alive. If you're already showing up in your own life, playing and loving, and not stressed out, worried and angry all the time, you're spending time in your connected mind. You already understand what it's like to be dead, though that's just part of the experience. To really explain what it's like to be dead, I'd like to tell you about a friend of mine, we'll call Bradley, who best answered the question "What's it like to be dead" for me, and in doing so, helped me truly see for the first time what it's like to be alive.

A few years ago, not long after I'd decided to try and explain the mechanics of being psychic and write a book, Bradley passed away. He was a trauma surgeon and a very special man who touched and saved the lives of many. His passing was a loss the entire community felt. The morning of his funeral, he showed up at my house. He was excited, but still a little thrown by the unexpected persistence of his consciousness. As a medical doctor, part of him was absolutely sure that his consciousness existed only because of and in his brain, and the logical, doctor part of his mind hadn't expected that he would exist after death. He appreciated the new freedom and abilities he had and was totally stoked to talk about his experience.

What Bradley loved most was that he was free of the confines of the body, and even more so, his brain. When we got in the car to go to the funeral, Bradley jumped in the backseat. He shared with me that his experience was that his brain had actually slowed his mind remarkably and being free of it was a wonderful relief, like a weight had been lifted. He could now get answers to questions just by wondering about the question or subject. He could not only travel wherever he wanted just by thinking about where he wanted to go, he also found that he had instantaneous access to any information or understanding he wanted, and no subject seemed to be out of reach or over his head. Like Google only way better!

Bradley's perspective let me firmly put the pieces of the psychic puzzle together and let go of all the baggage, stories, fears, judgements, and half-truths that science, religion and pop culture have projected onto what is just a basic human ability. When I could finally see the raw ability clearly, I started to see and feel for the first time in my life what it is really like to be human, and I could also clearly see how we have been taught to be afraid of who we are and our basic wiring. I used to explain that to access psychic information, I would alter my state through meditation and create a blank space in my mind. From this state, where part of me was 'one with everything' I would wonder about whatever or whoever I wanted to know about. Information and understandings about whatever I wondered about would then instantaneously pop into this blank space in my mind, as if I was directly connected to whatever or whomever I was wondering about.

The way Bradley described death to me was exactly like my experience of getting psychic information, and exactly how I did what I did as a telepath. It also explained why dead people provide such good advice, and why psychic information during my sessions often came from the dead people I was talking to, rather than me having had to look for it during mediumship sessions.[2] Bradley had inadvertently given me the best answer I had ever thought of to the question "How do you do what you do?". Finally, thanks to Bradley, I had an explanation that really made sense: I am just bringing awareness to the part of my mind that dead people live in, and we all have. I'm not doing anything special or unusual, I'm just freeing myself from my brain and my survivor mind momentarily, and using a part of my mind that we all have and will all return to: my connected mind.

In your connected mind, everything is just a thought away. You're connected to everything, all at once. You can relax in calm awareness and enjoy the feeling of connection, or you can focus on something – a person, place or thing – and get intimate information about any aspect of what you're focusing on. It's almost as if you momentarily become the thing you're focusing on; like you understand it from the inside. When you're fully in this part of your mind, it always feels safe and familiar; you just know that everything is going to be okay; that *you* will be okay. To get details about anything, you merely wonder about it, or who you want to talk to and you connect with it or them on a level that is best described as knowing, or what I call *clairiscience*. You don't get word answers, it's more like information comes in blocks or thought bubbles that contain all sorts of details, like the connection is mind-to-mind or mind-to-source: communication happens through your inner senses.

In more new age terms, you connect to the energy of someone or something; how it feels in its totality. It's information without words, raw information that needs to be translated as well as contextualized for it to make sense or be useful. It's not always easy to decipher and understand what you're looking at with your connected mind or what it relates to, let alone what it means. It's a skill that can be remembered, since it's an ability we all naturally possess but have forgotten how to use. The real challenge is distinguishing your connected mind from your survivor mind's projections, judgements and beliefs about how it thinks and imagines things should be, a challenge that becomes more and more difficult the more you try.

This book is not about convincing anyone that there is a connected mind, you know this place. You may already know this place really well, and seek it out regularly without consciously noticing or being able to explain the experience. Everyone on the planet spends some time in their connected mind, or has mastered using it in a particular way. Anytime you lose yourself doing something you love, when time seems to fly by, or slow down, when details or connections jump into sharp focus, everything is suddenly clear, you are in your connected mind. You've probably had many such moments, on a quiet nature walk, maybe cooking, painting, drawing or acting on stage, having a meaningful heart to heart with someone, playing a sport, or maybe while running or doing yoga. Almost all of us know this place, and intuitively seek it out for pleasure, to feel peace, or solve problems, but for the most part, we don't have the slightest inkling what's possible when we bring consciousness and skill to this place.

Learning about the connected mind can help you accomplish the extraordinary in life, the arts, athletics or business and can open the doorways to developing your own siddhis, or mind powers, but that's not really what this book is about. More than anything, it is about accepting and playing in the connected mind. I want to share what I've discovered and, in doing so, give you a new lens through which to see the world, and maybe your life.

To start, before I explain my personal experience of the connected mind, how to access your own, and what you'll find when you do, I have to address the biggest barriers most people face in accepting and understanding telepathic abilities:

- Mistaken identity – the belief that you are your body, and that your mind is the product of nerve activity in your brain (and is therefore stuck within your skull, isolated from the world except through the physical senses, and will cease to exist with the demise of the body).
- Materialism – the belief that nothing other than physical matter exists and that anything that cannot be explained

by the interactions of material things is impossible.
- Overconfident modernism – the belief that modern science (or any one book) has all the answers, and that we know pretty much all there is to know about the universe, the body, the brain, and the human condition.
- Fear of the unknown, which masquerades mostly as denial and dismissal in modern society.

To understand telepathy, and eventually get you back into your own telepathic abilities, there is a lot to unlearn. We have all experienced a surprisingly vast number of little moments over the years that have deeply implanted limiting beliefs into our psyches; beliefs that keep us out of connection and can be hard to let go of. It's surprising how visceral and irrational our reactions can be when we are first faced with undeniable evidence of the reality and power of telepathic abilities, or have our own connected mind experiences.

Initially, it all seems like magic, which many of us have been trained to fear. It's time to stop living in the dark ages though, time to stop fearing, persecuting and denying the existence of everything we don't yet understand. To do so, we're going to have to get a little uncomfortable while we look at some science, explained from a telepath's perspective, to unravel some of the deeply held beliefs we've all absorbed through school, the media and little moments over the years. It's important information that should not be glossed over, but feel free to read this book in any order you are inspired to, and skip to *Part II – The Connected Mind* if the unlearning gets to be too uncomfortable. Don't give up too quickly though. Remember, you are far, far more intelligent than conventional wisdom would have you believe (as you will soon find out), and in your connected mind, nothing is beyond your understanding. Any understanding you desire is accessible when you let yourself slip into connection, gently wonder, and follow your curiosity.

A No Brainer

If you want to know where you are, ask the non-locals.
~ Michael Talbot, *The Holographic Universe*

When it comes to abilities like mediumship, animal telepathy and psychic knowing, most rational, intelligent people who have not had spontaneous experiences of their own are skeptical. Ironically, this very skepticism is what prevents people from noticing their own connected minds and accessing their own extraordinary abilities. We tend to be skeptical of extraordinary abilities because we can't reconcile these abilities with our fundamental understanding of ourselves and our place in the universe: we almost universally believe that our minds are in our brains. If our minds are in our brains, isolated within our skulls, only able to interact with the wider world through our bodies and physical senses, it stands to logic that it's impossible to know things without seeing or hearing them directly. It is also impossible for dead people to talk through a medium, or even exist after their physical brain ceases to function since, when the body dies, the mind should cease to exist.

To most people, the idea that the mind is not in the brain is preposterous. We, of course, look out at the world with our eyes, from a perspective of somewhere inside our own head, and we all know that when the brain dies, we die, so of course our minds must be in our brains. Thanks to 200 years of neuroscience, we also have a fairly detailed understanding of the nervous system and which parts of the brain do what. With modern technology like functional MRIs and PET scanners that let researchers watch blood flow in the brain and see which parts of the brain 'light up' when we dream, meditate, or perform specific tasks, researchers can watch the brain in action. The brain imaging, models and theories we've devised to explain how the brain works are very convincing. It seems like a no brainer that we, and our minds, are in our brains. But should we believe the hype?

Many doctors and neuroscientists still admit that there is a lot about the brain we don't understand yet, and many mysteries yet to be solved. But what if there is far more (and far less) going on in the brain than most doctors and scientists are even willing to conceive of, let alone look for? Could brain scans and MRI images of the brain only be showing us a small part of what is actually going on in the human mind and brain? What if most researchers aren't willing to entertain let alone investigate bigger questions such as "Where is the mind?" because such questions are too complicated, open too big a can of worms, or are considered unscientific, unprovable, or traditionally fall into the realm of religion or philosophy?

What if the perspective from which we see the world is just that, a perspective, and not a true indication of where we are? What if our minds are not in our brains at all and the brain is actually more of an antenna, a receiver and transmitter, connecting our minds and consciousness to our bodies and the physical world, rather than an organ giving rise to our minds? Could doctors and scientists tell the difference between blood flowing to a specific part of the brain because thought is being produced there, versus the reception or transmission of thoughts, when they fiercely criticize or dismiss out of hand anyone who suggests that thought is not the mere product of brain function? What if the brain is more like a radio than a bio-computer? We can begin to understand how a radio works by observing and fiddling with the electronics inside, removing or damaging various parts of it and observing how the sound coming out of the radio changes, but we will never discover the source of the music if we only look inside the radio and never consider that the source of the music may be elsewhere.

Although they aren't yet household names, there are a number of brave doctors, neuroscientists and physicists who have compiled significant evidence and produced models and theories that explain how our brains function as a sort of antenna, and how this antenna or back door in space-time within our brains is connected to our consciousness, minds and the basic structure of the universe. In doing so, they have confirmed scientifically that our minds are not isolated in our brains and have started to answer questions like "Where are our minds?" and "How are our minds connected to one another, and everything else?". Although still controversial, as most revolutionary ideas are at first, evidence is mounting, theories are being refined and research into human consciousness, sometimes referred to as *pseudoscience* by the mainstream scientific community, is gradually being accepted into the realm of 'real' science.

As revolutionary as these emerging theories are, they don't actually contradict more conventional theories that model the brain as a sort of bio-computer isolated within our skulls. Rather, these models, which include holonomic brain theory, quantum mind theories and the morphic resonance hypothesis, complement conventional models of brain function. Fitting together like pieces in a puzzle, they answer questions that conventional models of the brain can't, and connect conventional models of the brain to our actual experience of the world: to consciousness and perception. By linking our brains and consciousness to the basic structure of the universe, these models and theories also explain why phenomena like telepathy, which have been labeled impossible or paranormal by the scientific community for decades, are perfectly possible, entirely normal and are in fact universal to all life.

The doctor and scientist who, to my knowledge, first put the pieces of the connected mind-brain puzzle together is Karl Pribram. Pribram is best known for defining the brain's limbic system and for developing holonomic brain theory. He held professorships at Georgetown University, Stanford and Yale over his distinguished career.[3] Among the first certified brain surgeons in the world, Pribram pioneered the field of neuropsychology, a term he invented.

Early in his career as a neurosurgeon, Pribram was charged with removing brain tumors. In a time before CAT scans and MRI brain imaging, Pribram was trained to deduce the location of brain tumors by observing the behavioral changes tumors caused in his patients. As the location of many tumors could be deduced by the effects a tumor was having on a patient's behavior, Pribram believed, as early anatomists did, and most people do today, that thought, perception and volition all occur in different parts of the brain, in spatially separated modules that we can define, name and surgically remove. This view was however challenged when Pribram began work as a research neurosurgeon with Harvard professor and neuropsychologist Karl Lashley in 1946.

Lashley, who had spent 30 years studying the effects of brain damage, systematically searching for the location memories are stored in the brain, and not finding one, had come to a very different conclusion about the brain. In early experiments, Lashley trained lab rats to run a maze for food, then systemically severed or cut out parts of their brains to determine in which part of the brain stored their memories. No matter what part of the brain he cut out though, his rats always remembered their way through mazes they had learned to navigate. Even rats whose ability to walk was impaired after having large portions of their brains removed still managed to wobble down familiar pathways.

Lashley found that his rats' ability to problem solve was impaired in proportion to the amount of brain tissue he removed, but the location of the brain damage was essentially irrelevant and he could not cut out his rats' memories. In later experiments, Lashley and other investigators were able to show that removing thin sections of brain tissue has little to no effect on memory or behavior. Their experiments showed that nerve impulses still travel across severed sections of nerves in the brain, and that the exact pathways nerve impulses take across the brain doesn't seem to matter.

Lashley felt his findings showed that the brain operates primarily as a single, undifferentiated unit, with memory and brain function spread out over the entire brain rather than occurring in separate modules. Furthermore, Lashley felt that brain activity depended on the pattern of mass excitation of nerve cells within general regions of the brain, but not on which nerve cells in particular fire, or the specific pathways nerve impulses followed. Lashley's intuition, which turned out to be uncannily accurate, was that perception and memory functioned through electrical activity that occurs over the entire brain, in the form of interfering waves of electricity, what we now commonly refer to as brain waves.

Experiments with salamanders, intended to disprove Lashley's whole brain idea, were even more baffling than Lashley's experiments with rats. Salamanders are remarkable creatures and the subject of ongoing scientific study today because they heal perfectly without any scarring whatsoever. Salamanders can also regenerate severed spinal cords, limbs, organs, and brain tissue. Salamanders even survive having their entire brains surgically removed, and then later replaced.

Removing a salamander's brain, expectedly, puts it into a state of stupor. Salamanders, however, return to normal behavior in time, seemingly no worse for wear, if their brains are returned to their heads. In the early 1960s, biologist Paul Pietsch took advantage of this ability to explore how the brain stores memories. In an effort to disprove the idea that memories are stored over the entire brain, Pietsch taught salamanders how to navigate mazes for food; then, surgically removed their brains and replaced them upside down, or dissected with pieces interchanged. Pietsch hypothesized that if memories were stored non-locally over salamanders' entire brains, then salamanders would still be able to access their memories after having their brains shuffled.

In his book *Shufflebrain,* Pietsch explains how he performed some 700 brain shuffling operations on salamanders. Initially he had expected his salamanders to remain in a state of stupor or behave strangely after having their brains shuffled, thus disproving the theory that memories are stored over the entire brain. To his surprise, however, his salamanders not only returned to normal behavior again and again after having their brains removed then replaced upside down, dissected, jumbled and even whipped into mush in a blender, they also remembered paths through mazes they had learned to navigate prior to their brain shuffling operations! Dramatic evidence to Pietsch that memories and the mind are somehow spread out over the entire brain in a manner such that the mind is preserved, even when the nerve cells and the connections that were thought to encode memories and cognition are jumbled or destroyed.

To more open-minded or spiritual observers, the observation that salamanders remember mazes and return to normal behavior after their brains have been literally turned to mush is clear evidence that salamanders' memories and minds aren't in their material brains at all. If memories were stored in the structure or order of salamanders' physical brains, then when Pietsch's salamanders grew new brains (from the shuffled remnants of their old brains) their new brains should have been blank slates. If, however, the mind of a salamander is thought of as a field that occupies the brain, a nonphysical structure around which the cells in a salamander's body and brain organize themselves, then it is easy to imagine that Pietsch's salamanders' brain cells simply re-formed around their nonphysical minds. The exact order and placement that shuffled brain cells took wouldn't matter, because salamanders' minds aren't in their brain cells. The brain simply forms a structure through which salamanders' nonphysical minds can perceive the physical world and communicate with their physical bodies.

Of course, brain recovery in salamanders may not seem to have anything to do with fragile human brains. The human brain is, however, surprisingly resilient to localized trauma, and it is well-known to neurosurgeons that people can and do survive having large sections of their brains removed, or damaged, often with surprisingly little effect on personality or memory. Medical literature is full of cases of patients walking into emergency rooms, fully conscious and talking, with knives, branches, rebar or bullets lodged across entire sections of their brains.

Severe epilepsy is still treated today by surgically removing parts of the brain. In very severe cases in young children, doctors completely remove half of the brain. Amazingly, children who have large portions of their brains removed in early childhood still display normal intelligence, and there is little long-term effect on their memories or personalities. Hemispherectomies, the surgical removal of half of the brain, have been performed on hundreds of children to treat severe epilepsy, children who have returned to more normal lives after the procedure, and in fact have typically performed better in school after the surgery.

Doctors typically explain the miraculous recoveries people make after severe brain injury by suggesting that the brain reorganizes itself, and that the remaining parts of an injured brain take over for the missing parts. This is a seeming reasonable explanation until you consider how the remaining parts of an injured brain could possibly know what parts are missing, how to take over for them, and how to reorganize: if the mind was in the physical brain, then missing or damaged parts of the brain should result in the corresponding permanent loss of part of the mind. Perhaps we are not so different from salamanders after all.[4]

After working with Lashley, Pribram went on to become a professor at Yale University where he continued to ponder the contradiction between Lashley's *whole brain* idea and the ongoing obsession of brain researchers (that continues today) with mapping the brain by correlating experience and behavior with specific locations of brain activity or damage. Pribram felt that the contradictory maps of brain function various investigators had produced over the years, and the immensely complex relationships he was discovering between the brain and behavior, suggested that: "brain mapmaking, even when carefully based on sustainable correlations, was not sufficient to constitute a science. Just because we can show by electrical recording or by clinical or surgical damage that a select place in the brain is involved in color vision does not mean that it is *the* or even a 'center' for processing color."[5] Pribram began looking beyond the shape and structure of the brain for more complex patterns of brain function, focusing on perception, and how the brain translates nerve impulses from the eyes into moving electric fields in the brain.

As Pribram pioneered new ways to record and study electrical activity in the brain, he came across a *Scientific American* article on the emerging science of holography, in which two optical engineers described how they had been able to store an immense number of three-dimensional images on a single piece of film by recording images as interference patterns, rather than as photographic images. The article explained how laser light could be reflected off three-dimensional objects, and captured as an interference pattern on film. Illuminating the film with the same laser, at exactly the same angle as the laser used to illuminate each object, produced a hologram of the object – a perfect three-dimensional image of the original object that appeared in thin air. By illuminating objects with a laser at different angles, many holograms could be encoded on, and reproduced from, a single film.

The article explained that though *holographs* (the term I use for the surfaces or films that holograms are captured on, just as we refer to photographic films as photographs) could encode hundreds of images, they just looked like blurred lines and water stains. Holograms were captured and stored as interference patterns spread over the *entire* surface of holographic films. If a holograph was cut in half, or many pieces, the holograms stored on the film could still be reproduced in their entirety from each piece of the film, just with less detail.[6]

To understand how holographs encode information, you can think of a holographic film like a still pond. If you throw rocks into a still pond, the concentric ripples each rock makes will spread over the entire pond. All the ripples will add together, or cancel out, all over the pond, forming an interference pattern across the entire surface of the pond. The pattern of interfering waves on any part of the pond will contain enough information about every rock thrown into the pond that, given enough time and some math skills (or perceptive ability), one could reconstruct a picture of the size of each rock thrown into the pond, and the time at which each rock hit the water. Holographic films encode 3D holographic images much like a pond encodes information about rocks thrown into it.

Reading the article, in a flash, Pribram realized that the brain must store memories in the same way, which explained why Lashley had not been able to cut memories out of the mind by cutting out pieces of the brain. Holographic memory storage also explained why his patients woke from brain surgery with 'fuzzy' memories, but never 'chunks' or sections of their memories missing. He also realized exactly what the electric fields and interference patterns he and Lashley had been studying in the brain for years were: holographically encoded interference patterns. Pribram realized that holographic storage and processing might be the key to understanding how the brain processes and stores information, and he set out to investigate his hypothesis.

As Pribram explored the idea and gathered evidence, he

realized that understanding the brain as a holographic organ explained a number of mysteries about the brain and consciousness:

- the complex electrical impulses he and other scientists could measure and observe travelling through the brain;
- the enormity of human memory capacity given the size of our brains;
- our ability to pick familiar faces out of a large crowd, and recognize people at different ages;[7]
- why memories are so strongly associated with one another, smells or tastes;
- why our brains process sensory stimuli such as sound and light as frequencies;
- how our brain creates the illusion of the world we see 'out there': our brains trick us into believing that electrical impulses in our brains are objects 'out there' in the real world. The world we see 'out there' is not the actual world. It is our brains' translation of light, sound and kinetic energy from the world around us, energy that our brains translate into a hologram, inside our own heads, and sensations in our bodies – images and sensations that appear and feel so real, that we believe them to be the real world.

By the 1970s Pribram had accumulated enough evidence to convince himself that the brain does indeed store memories and processes information holographically. As Pribram's conception of the brain as a holographic lens grew, repeatedly thinking the idea through to its logical end, he kept coming to the same conclusion, and started to wonder if his research was pointing to something bigger. He began to realize that, without our physical senses and brains converting light, sound and kinetic energy into the hologram of the world we see in our minds and project out onto the world, we would be immersed in a holographic experience: we might experience the world more like an interference pattern on a holographic film rather than its three-dimensional projection.

The question that bothered Pribram the most was that: if our brains reconstruct the picture of objective reality we see in a way similar to how a hologram is reconstructed from an interference pattern on a holographic film, then what does that say about physical reality? The only logical conclusion his holographic model of the brain kept leading him to was the same conclusion that Eastern traditions had been teaching for millennia: *that the world of separate objects we see with our eyes is maya – the illusion of reality created through the perspective of our physical senses.*

The world out there exists as we see it, but also in a way that we cannot perceive through our physical senses, as a vast, interconnected, resonating symphony of energy: an immense holograph in which objects we perceive as separate are actually spread across the universe as intermingled, interfering waves of energy. Like a holographic film, the entire universe would be reflected in, and connected to, every other part, and, every part of the universe would be *informed* by every other part.

Realizing that the answers to his questions went well beyond biology, but might be found in the physics of holograms, Pribram sought the help of his son, who happened to be a physicist. Pribram's son informed him that another rather well-known physicist, David Bohm, through his research in quantum physics, had already come to the conclusion that the entire universe functions as a sort of living hologram: a holographic universe in which Pribram's holographic brain theory fit like a missing puzzle piece.

Fear, Magic and a Second Level of Reality

> *It isn't that the world of appearances is wrong, it isn't that there aren't objects out there, at one level of reality. It's that if you penetrate through and look at the universe with a holographic system, you arrive at a different view, a different reality. And that other reality can explain things that have hitherto remained inexplicable scientifically: paranormal phenomena, synchronicities, the apparently meaningful coincidence of events.*
> ~ Karl Pribram

The idea that there are two levels of reality goes back a very long way, and was probably self-evident to most of humanity, for most of history. Every culture on the planet throughout history has acknowledged a second level of reality in some form: as a spirit world, realm of the gods, heaven or underworld. The more primitive and connected to nature a culture is, the more important and direct its interactions and relationships with a second level of reality tend to be. Early humans living in nature, judging by what we know of them today, very much appear to have lived in two worlds, paying attention to spirits and spirit worlds as much as the physical world, and nurturing very real relationships with non-physical aspects of themselves, the animals they hunted, the ecosystems around them, as well as the stars and their ancestors in many cases.

Although we might dismiss such ideas and experiences as silly fantasies made up by primitive peoples who didn't know any better, considering how new the idea that physical reality is the only reality, perhaps we should be asking the question: Which culture is the delusional one? Every culture in history that came before us, or ours? With none of the distractions of hurried modern life, little focus on conceptual or intellectual thinking, and daily access to altered states of consciousness that modern life keeps most present day humans from experiencing, our so-called primitive ancestors may well have been far more advanced in their ability to access and navigate altered states of consciousness than most of us are today.

Modern science began to bump up against a second level of reality in the early 1900s with the advent of quantum physics. The problem physicists initially faced was the wave-particle duality of light. Light travels as a wave that behaves very much like waves on water do by:

- spreading out and travelling as a *front* that follows every path on a trajectory, rather than taking one single path through space as an object or particle would,
- bending when it is slowed down by air, water or encounters obstacles, and
- creating interference patterns where light waves cancel each other out (creating dark spots) or add to one another (creating bright spots).

Light, however, also behaves as if it is a particle, hitting individual atoms or molecules and leaving dots on photographic films for example, as if light particles hit photographic films one by one like muddy tennis balls hitting a white wall. In 1905, Albert Einstein proposed that light was both a wave and a particle, and summed up the problem stating that: "we have two contradictory pictures of reality; separately, neither of them fully explains the phenomena of light, but together they do." By 1924, French physicist Louis de Broglie had shown that electrons, previously thought to be particles, also had wave-like properties. He then expanded the 'two pictures of reality' problem by proposing that all matter has wave-like properties.

De Broglie's work led to the formulation of quantum mechanics, which is still considered, along with general relativity, to be the most successful quantitative scientific theory ever devised. Quantum mechanics has allowed physicists to understand, predict and model the world to extraordinary degrees of precision. It has been used to invent and engineer most modern technology from lasers, to microwaves, to microchips, to MRI scanners, to cell phones and flat screen TVs. In the 1920s, quantum mechanics provided a huge leap in physicists' ability to understand and predict the behavior of the physical world. However, the same equations that allowed physicists to predict the behavior of light, energy, quantum particles and matter with such incredible precision also described 'two contradictory pictures of reality', and a second, nonphysical reality that worked in very, very strange ways.

The wave function, the equation that describes how quantum systems work, requires an observer. Observer and quantum particles are very intimately linked. According to quantum mechanics, quantum particles behave in entirely different ways when they are being observed, and when they are not observed. When not observed, quantum particles don't behave like separate objects flying on specific paths through space at all. Rather, quantum mechanics describes particles spreading out into *superposition,* simultaneously taking every possible path they can through space, and spreading out through space and time, into the future, and the past. In superposition, quantum particles appeared to magically exist simultaneously in many places and many times, all at once. They also appeared to communicate with one another over large distances and across time.

In superposition, quantum particles seemed to be everywhere and nowhere all at once. Until they were observed, they seemed to be both everything they could possibly be, and nothing at all, existing in states of pure potential and possibility. Some physicists referred to the strange way in which matter seemed to exist when it wasn't being observed as *quantum foam* or *quantum soup,* because when not observed, matter seemed to behave more like an invisible liquid spread over all space; a medium in which every part was in touch with and affected by every other part.

Quantum particles seemed to travel through this strange soup much like waves on the ocean, but rather than waves of energy, quantum waves behaved more like waves of possibility. Quantum mechanics described the motion of particles in terms of the probabilities and possibilities rather than being in specific places and times. It also described an inherent amount of uncertainty in the world: an exact limit on how much you could know (and therefore predict) about any quantum particle's location and speed, known as Heisenberg's Uncertainty Principle. Rather than a deterministic universe, where everything unfolds according to exact equations and immutable laws, quantum mechanics pointed to a mysteriously unpredictable universe where chance, or some other mysterious and unknown force (possibly connected to an observer) played a fundamental role in each and every interaction of matter and energy.

The rabbit hole of superposition, matter-observer entanglement, inherent uncertainty and quantum soup that physicists found themselves staring into in the 1920s was so strange that the some of the same physicists who developed quantum theory decided to ignore the whole second picture of reality, observer-matter interaction, everywhere-nowhere problem altogether in what is called the *Copenhagen interpretation* of quantum mechanics. In the Copenhagen interpretation, the founding fathers of quantum mechanics declared that quantum theory was complete, and that it was meaningless to talk about quantum particles in superposition, because particles in superposition didn't really exist. They declared that the equations that described quantum particles in superposition "did not yield a description of objective reality."

In other words, the founding fathers of quantum physics decided that half of the most successful quantitative scientific theory of all time should be ignored altogether because it didn't seem to make sense. This fearful reaction and refusal to consider, let alone investigate, the meaning of revolutionary scientific findings by the very scientists who contributed to the discovery is quite understandable, given the magical reality quantum mechanics pointed to, and the deep seated fear of magic that has pervaded Western thought for several millennia.

Looking back over history, a powerful and visceral fear of magic seems to have arisen in our collective consciousness with the advent of agriculture and civilization. When we began to grow our own food, and live and die by our own hands, hard work, or lack thereof, we left the proverbial Garden of Eden, where, as hunter-gatherers, nature provided all for us. Rather than a trusted abundant giving mother whose bounty could be found everywhere if you followed her signs and your instincts, Mother Nature became a cagey business partner. Mother Nature's love or wrath meant years of plenty or the decimation of entire crops, and the loss of months of toil and backbreaking work that went into their cultivation. We gradually stopped trusting the magic of nature to provide for us, and our connection to nature, and we began to plot, calculate and hoard to outwit Mother Nature and maximize her output.

We staked our claims on plots of land and fought to keep nature away, weeds out of our fields and animals as well as other humans from stealing our crops. We came to rely on our own strength, hard work, knowledge and logical decision-making skills rather than instinct and intuition. We began to see Mother Earth as a conditionally loving provider and began to live with worries about the future and dividing or controlling limited resources more than the abundance of the present moment. Our focus turned to building and defending property and the spoils of our labor. We gradually left our telepathic connection to everything around us, and rather than living in the moment and trusting our connected minds to guide and inform us, we began living more and more in our plotting, mistrusting, conceptual survivor minds.

With productive property and jealous neighbors also came the possibility that the fertility of one's land and the products of one's hard labor could be magically charmed away. Laws against magic go back as far as Plato and early Greek law, in which records can be found of farmers having to defend themselves in court against accusations that their bountiful harvests were the result of magically charming away the fertility of their neighbors' land. Greek laws against magic can be followed into Roman law, and then into the Catholic Church, through which the fear of magic became institutionalized, more irrational, and more elaborate. Fear turned into widespread persecution during the Spanish Inquisition and *the burning times*, during which the fear of magic saw tens if not hundreds of thousands, mostly women, burned at the stake. Misogyny and the fear of magic, long associated with the divine feminine, are intimately linked.

It's been almost two hundred years since the last public witch burning in Europe, but an irrational, visceral fear of magic still burns brightly in our collective consciousness, even among many of the supposed rational leaders in the scientific community. It's been less than 30 years since the editor of *Nature*, arguably the most prestigious scientific journal in the world, declared a book titled *A New Science of Life* by Cambridge biologist Rupert Sheldrake: an "infuriating tract… the best candidate for [book] burning there has been for many years" and that "Sheldrake [was] putting forward magic instead of science, and that can be condemned in exactly the language that the Pope used to condemn Galileo,[8] and for the same reason. It is heresy."

Sheldrake's infuriating hypothesis (based on scientific observation, experimentation and thorough research) was simply that informed action at a distance plays a key role in biology and cellular processes. The public burnings may have stopped, but the threats of burning and irrational public persecution of anything perceived as magical have continued through to the present day – though mostly in more benign forms such as denial, shunning and public dismissal of anyone who actually believes (beyond faith) in a second level of reality or phenomenon that can't be easily explained through material means. Discrimination on the basis of race, religion and sexual orientation is unacceptable in most circles in the 21st century; discrimination and bullying of anyone who doesn't fit into a materialist paradigm, however, remains our societal norm.

The widespread assumption in most of modern society continues to be that anyone who actually believes, beyond faith, in knowing or action at a distance, non-physical realities or non-physical causes must be deluded or crazy, and that it is okay to publicly judge, ridicule, discredit or dismiss such people. On a personal level, I am still amazed at the fear that even smart, educated, theoretically open-minded people react with at times when confronted with something they can't explain. Even some of my clients, who have arranged and paid for sessions completely out of their own volition, react with fear when we begin, or when validations that prove the reality of the experience beyond any reasonable doubt start coming through.

Though the fear of magic, and persecution it elicits, mostly masquerades as denial and other relatively benign forms of social ostracism today, there are more serious implications. I cringe to think how many telepathically gifted but troubled and misunderstood people have been locked up in hospitals, pharmacologically numbed into compliant zombies, or have endured intrusive and painful medical procedures at the hands of well-meaning professionals acting out of an institutionalized, irrational fear of magic. Collectively, I don't think we are anywhere near as enlightened as we would like to believe we are, and in many ways, we have barely left the dark ages.

Although a number of notable physicists, including Albert Einstein, swiftly rejected the Copenhagen interpretation of quantum mechanics after it was proposed, the Copenhagen interpretation became the dominant view among most physicists, and was regarded as the *standard interpretation* for most of the 20th century. Citing the standard interpretation, any exploration as to:

- why an observer is needed in quantum equations;
- how the human mind might act as an observer and interact with matter; or
- the idea that a second reality exists

has largely been declared pseudoscience, quantum mysticism or meaningless speculation by mainstream scientists for nearly a century. The dismissive environment has created an intolerance towards 'spiritual' people who intuitively know such things to be true. Worse, it has all but stopped the scientific investigation of human consciousness and related research, and skewed research funding to our collective detriment. We cannot hope to solve humanity's pressing problems if we collectively ignore half of reality and, along with it, half of the human condition.

In a 1935 paper outlining what is known as the EPR paradox, Einstein, along with fellow physicists Podolsky and Rosen, famously and publicly aired their concern with the Copenhagen interpretation. Einstein and his colleagues pointed out that the Copenhagen formulation of quantum mechanics violated the theory of relativity. According to the theory of relativity, it is impossible to accelerate any object, no matter how small, to the speed of light. Quantum mechanics, which the Copenhagen interpretation declared was a complete theory, described quantum particles in certain situations, instantaneously communicating with one another, regardless of distance. This type of communication between quantum particles is referred to as *non-local* (independent of location) action at a distance. Einstein felt that, in order for entangled quantum particles to communicate with one another, some sort of signal had to travel between the particles. Since quantum mechanics described instantaneous communication regardless of distance, the signal would have to travel faster than the speed of light, violating the theory of relativity.

Einstein described non-local communication between quantum particles as "spooky action at a distance", words that subtly reveal the long-standing and deeply ingrained fear of unmediated action at a distance, or magic, in the scientific community. The EPR paradox framed the debate around quantum physics for decades to come in terms of non-locality, whether one part of the universe can be instantaneously connected to and informed by what is happening in another part of the universe – a debate that entirely sidestepped the bigger existential issue quantum mechanics raised: the existence of a second level of reality.

From a telepath's perspective, Einstein's discomfort with quantum mechanics and "spooky action at a distance" is both interesting and ironic. Einstein is famous for his thought experiments, experiments in which he would get lost in his 'imagination' for hours, doing such things as imagining himself as a beam of light. Einstein relates coming back from his thought experiments with answers to his questions about physics and the nature of reality, and credits his ideas for the theory of relativity to one such thought experiment. Some of his better-known quotes include: "The only real valuable thing is intuition," and "Imagination is more important than knowledge." To me, it is very clear that Einstein was a gifted telepath, and very comfortable entering altered states for hours, in which he could find and bring back intuitive understandings and psychic information about the nature of the universe – intuitive understandings that he then described mathematically.

Einstein's intuitive discomfort with Copenhagenism, an ideal that placed a taboo on exploring the aspects of quantum physics that explain why his thought experiments worked so well, is not surprising. It is ironic that Einstein chose to try and discredit Copenhagenism by pointing out that it permitted informed action at a distance – the very means through which I would suggest his much valued intuition and thought experiments functioned. Irony is, however, a telltale sign of the connected mind at work, and a sign of Einstein's brilliance as a telepath in this case: irony is a form of synchronicity, or meaningful coincidence. Rather than the meaning of an event being synchronistically or serendipitously aligned with a thought, purpose or intention, the actual meaning of an ironic event is the opposite of that intended. The connected mind functions through focus, whether that focus is positive or negative, and irony and synchronicities are two sides of the same coin. So, although experiments conducted after Einstein's death have shown that action at a distance does occur, contrary to Einstein's discomfort, his intuitive understanding that something was wrong with Copenhagenism was bang on, even if he couldn't pinpoint exactly why.

Today, there are fourteen plus interpretations of quantum mechanics, all of which imply different things about the nature of the universe and the human mind. One of the central distinctions among the interpretations is whether superposition and the wave nature of matter is real, or not. The question is usually phrased in terms of what the *wave-function*, the equation that describes the behavior of quantum particles, represents, and whether the wave-function is a mathematical illusion, or represents something real, that actually exists.

The Copenhagen interpretation finally began to lose its hegemonic popularity among physicists in the early 21st century, and the news headlines coming out of the physics world have become much more interesting as a result. The *many worlds* or *multiverse* interpretation has gained popularity, possibly due to Stephen Hawking's advocacy of the idea. The many worlds interpretation proposes that superposition represents infinite parallel universes – universes just like ours that each take different paths through history, all existing at once.

Quantum information or *it from bit* approaches, originally

proposed by physicist John Wheeler, that contend that information is the fundamental building block of the universe have also gained popularity. Such theories suggest that information lies at the core of every particle, every field of force, and spacetime itself, an idea that, from a telepath's perspective, makes total sense and goes a long way in explaining what telepaths, psychics and shamans perceive in altered states, and the nature of the information they bring back. One of the earliest and elegantly simple interpretations of quantum mechanics, that has, in many ways, stood the test of time, also closely matches my experience of telepathic reality: pilot wave theory, also known as de Broglie–Bohm theory.

In Louis de Broglie's 1924 thesis, which led to the development of quantum mechanics and for which he received the Nobel Prize, de Broglie did away with the concept of wave-particle duality. Instead, de Broglie conceived of matter-waves as connected, indivisible entities, wherein the behavior and movement of quantum particles is informed and guided by invisible *pilot waves*. David Bohm expanded de Broglie's matter-wave theory into an interpretation of quantum mechanics in 1952. In de Broglie–Bohm theory, quantum matter-waves exist all the time, rather than existing in multiple universes, or vanishing into nonexistence when not observed, then collapsing back into particles of physical matter when observed as the Copenhagen interpretation contends.

De Broglie–Bohm theory describes the behavior and movement of matter-waves in an equation that essentially depends on the configuration of the entire universe. Nothing is separate. All matter-waves in the universe are connected to, informed, and influenced by the state of all other matter-waves in the universe through an invisible information field of interacting pilot waves (represented by the wave function) that exist in a second level of reality. This second level of reality, a deeper and more fundamental order of existence than the physical world, is non-local: it is everywhere yet in no specific location or time. It pervades, infuses and informs all space, matter and time – thus connecting all matter and all points in space and time.

When David Bohm came across holography, he recognized the striking similarity between the physics of pilot waves, and the physics of holograms. He quickly became convinced that matter-waves, and the universe itself, actually function through holographic principles: that matter-waves constitute a giant holograph, a second, more immense and fundamental level of reality that is projected onto space and time to give rise to the physical universe, which is a kind of giant, moving hologram. Bohm, recognizing that the hologram metaphor provided tremendous insight into how the universe works, dubbed this second level of reality the *holomovement*.[9]

If we return to our still pond metaphor of a holograph, the holomovement encodes information about all matter in the universe, through all time, in a way similar to the way in which a still pond encodes information about rocks thrown into it. 'Echos' of every event in our lives and throughout history are recorded in the holomovement, preserving information about the near and distant past. I believe we find ourselves in the holomovement, or subtle reality as I refer to it, when we withdraw our focus from our physical bodies and senses, or die.

If you were to spend enough time throwing rocks into ponds and watching the ripples, or filming rocks being thrown into ponds and watching the films in reverse, you might be able train your mind to accurately imagine the size and shape of rocks that will make, or have made, any given ripple pattern on a pond. This is metaphorically pretty much how I believe we can all learn telepathic abilities: by withdrawing our senses from physical reality, repeatedly, for short periods of time, to peer into holographic reality.

Holography gives us exacting insight as to how this process works and how the information we find in the holomovement relates to physical reality. Bohm suggests that the holomovement functions like a holographic projector, not just recording, but projecting information into the physical reality we see and experience through our senses, creating the cosmos, the present moment and the future. I believe that when we learn to access, orient ourselves in, and navigate the holomovement, we can begin to recognize the information that records and gives rise to physical reality, and learn to correlate that information with the physical world. Over time, we can become better and better at recognizing holographic information about the past, present and future, and understanding what it means.

Seeing a real hologram can help us understand how this process works, and can also help us break through limiting beliefs by showing us, in real life, on a micro scale, how information can exist in two dimensions and be projected into three dimensions. Unfortunately, most people today are only familiar with a type of hologram called a rainbow hologram, commonly found on children's toys and credit cards, and have not experienced the jaw dropping, walk around and view from multiple angles, reach out and touch, three-dimensional realism of a true hologram generated with lasers. When we look at a rainbow hologram at just the right angle, a very real looking three-dimensional image appears that can be viewed from many angles, just like a real object. Though rainbow holograms are impressive, their design makes compromises to permit them to be viewed under normal lighting conditions. Rainbow holograms aren't nearly as impressive or three-dimensionally real looking as true holograms generated with laser light.

To make a true hologram, a three-dimensional image made of light that literally appears in thin air, lasers are required. A beam of laser light is split. Part of the beam is used to illuminate an object, and the other part of the beam, the *reference beam,* is reflected around the object, towards a holographic film. The laser light that bounces off the illuminated object is recombined with the reference beam, and the interference pattern the two beams create is captured on film. A light field is captured, rather than a slice of points of light a photograph captures. The process is similar to sound recording where sound fields, containing spectrums of sound vibrations, are captured on a record, MP3 or compact disc. Just like sound recordings have to be played back through speakers to recreate the original sound, holographs must be 'played back' by illuminating a holograph with a *reconstruction* beam – a beam of the same laser light used to make the holograph, aimed at the holograph at exactly the same angle as the angle of the reference beam used to capture the holograph. When a reconstruction beam passes through a holograph, a hologram appears in thin air on the other side of the holograph.

There are two important things to understand about holography here. First, you can capture many different holograms on a single two-dimensional surface. Several thousand three-dimensional images can be stored on a surface or film by changing the angle of the reference beam used to capture each holograph. Each 3D hologram can be projected from the film by illuminating the film with laser light at the same angle as the reference beam used to record an object's holograph. In other words, what you see when you look at a hologram depends entirely on the perspective from which you illuminate the holograph that gives rise to it. A single holograph can produce thousands of completely different 3D holograms, which hologram you see depends entirely on the angle that you view (or illuminate) the holograph from.

Secondly, holographs are self-referential. They look the same at many scales and each part of a holograph encodes the entirety of all the holograms stored on it. If you cut a holographic film into pieces, no matter the shape or size of the pieces you cut, as long as there are enough 'ripples' to create an interference pattern, each piece of a holograph will still contain all the exact holograms as the original film, only blurrier with a slightly different angle of view. Each piece of a holographic film cut into parts can still be used to view all of the original images recorded on it.

I think of the focus of my consciousness in altered states as a sort of holographic reconstruction beam. When I withdraw my focus from physical reality, I believe that I find myself in the holomovement, or subtle reality as I call it. My focus and consciousness 'project' whatever I focus on in subtle reality into a sort of hologram in my mind. Information about anything and everything in the entire universe is theoretically available, as each part of subtle reality reflects the whole and contains information about the past, present and future. Finding the right 'perspective' or 'focus' to separate out and 'project' desired information from an infinite storehouse of information is the challenge. I believe that this ability is universal and the experience commonplace. Understood as 'overlays' of nonphysical realities, projected onto the holographic images in our minds we believe to be physical reality, a range of so-called hallucinations, visions, mystical and paranormal experiences can be readily explained and understood.

In David Bohm's conception, quantum physics describes the physical universe as a holographic projection of an immense underlying holograph – the holomovement – a word he coined to emphasize its dynamic, flowing nature. Bohm saw the holomovement giving rise to the physical universe, just as a holograph gives rise to a hologram, and the physical universe in a state of constant unfoldment from and enfoldment back into the holomovement. In the holomovement, all points in space converge and become one interconnected ocean of information and energy, on which an immense holographic interference pattern dances.

Just like a holographic film, each point in the holomovement contains the whole, and so every piece of matter in the universe is interconnected and informed by the state of the rest of the universe. Information giving rise to the past, present and future states of the physical world is 'encoded' in the holomovement, information that, like energy in the physical world, cannot be destroyed. I think this is why, as a telepath, I can obtain certain types of information about almost anything past, present or future.

When David Bohm met Karl Pribram, holonomic brain theory fit into Bohm's conception of the holomovement perfectly. The human mind now had a basis in physics, as a living holograph within the holomovement. Suddenly nothing, human beings and the human mind included, could be considered separate or isolated. The entire universe had to be considered as one interconnected whole, every part of which interacts with every other part through the holomovement. In the holomovement, consciousness and matter, both forms of holographically encoded information, would be essentially equivalent, and would interact with one another. Bohm proposed that consciousness could be understood as a subtler form of matter, an idea that physicists are now seriously exploring.

The human mind, existing as a dynamic holograph within the holomovement, could be said to exist in a second level of reality, a deeper, more fundamental reality existing outside of space and time as we know it. Bohm's physics and Pribram's biology pointed to human beings existing simultaneously in two realities: as material brains atop bodies in physical reality, arising from nonphysical minds encoded within the holomovement. As the physical world arises from the holomovement, not the other way around, and the holomovement encodes the past, present and future, the human mind could then be thought of as an immortal living holograph and the body its material expression. As part of the holomovement, the human mind would also be informed and influenced by the state of the rest of the entire universe, past, present and future, and would therefore be inherently and naturally telepathic.

Thinking Outside of the Brain

Inside all of us is Hope.
Inside all of us is Fear.
Inside all of us is Adventure.
Inside all of us is…A Wild Thing
…Let the wild rumpus start.
~ Maurice Sendak, *Where the Wild Things Are*

Working in collaboration with David Bohm, Karl Pribram developed his insight that the brain is a holographic organ into *holonomic brain theory*, which he fully described in his 1991 book *Brain and Perception*. Holonomic brain theory models the brain as a holographic storage network, where our memories and minds are encoded as interference patterns in waves of electricity that flow back and forth over our brains: our brain waves. Different parts of the brain convert nerve impulses from our body, skin, eyes and ears into electromagnetic waveforms and perform different functions in processing the waveforms, but the whole brain works as a single unit over which holographic waveforms are stored and manipulated.

As brilliant as Pribram's discovery was, it did not receive a lot of attention in the scientific community or mass media. The theory explained a number of mysteries about the brain, our consciousness and how the mind works, and even provided mathematical models through which aspects of consciousness and the mind could be understood; however, Pribram's theory was a quantum leap for the scientific community to digest. Holonomic brain theory wrenched the study of the mind away from the conventional biology and medicine and brought the study of the human mind firmly into the realm of quantum physics. Though the idea that quantum processes are somehow related to consciousness and the human mind had emerged with the advent of quantum physics in 1920s, the subject of what role, if any, quantum physics plays in the human mind remains rather taboo in the mainstream scientific community, where the concept is still dismissively referred to as *quantum mysticism.*

Although David Bohm is considered to be one of the most significant physicists of the 20th century, his work did not receive much attention in the mainstream media or scientific community either. He is acknowledged to have made significant contributions to physics, neuropsychology and the philosophy of mind, and although his work is considered creative, it has generally been considered unorthodox. His ideas have, however, stood the test of time. Around 1978, physicists again came across a second level of reality when what is known as the *holographic principle* emerged as a property of string theory.

String theory is now considered by many physicists to be the best candidate for a theory of everything[10] and the holographic principle, in its widest sense, suggests that the universe is a two-dimensional information structure 'projected' onto the three-dimensional cosmos we see with our eyes, just as in Bohm's conception. In Bohm's words, the universe is comprised of the two-dimensional holomovement, which gives rise to the three-dimensional physical universe.

String theory made a big leap forward in 1997 thanks to *the most reliable realization of the holographic principle to date* known as gauge/gravity correspondence. Formulated by theoretical physicist Juan Maldacena, the correspondence shows that a number of physics theories that describe gravity, previously thought to be incompatible with theories describing quantum physics, actually describe the same physics. The correspondence has allowed physicists to translate calculations back and forth between gravity theories, and quantum field theories. When gravitational theory is hard to solve, quantum field theory is easy to solve and vice versa.

Maldacena's discovery has led to continual advances in string theory since 1997, and each success has further validated the notion that we live in a holographic universe: quantum field theories require one less dimension than gravity theories, suggesting that quantum interactions take place in a dimension or reality with one less dimension than the physical world. News headlines like "The Universe Is a Hologram" or "Physicists Say We Live in a Computer Simulation" have appeared with some regularity as string theory has progressed. The implications of living in a holographic universe, however, never make the news and the profound significance of gauge/gravity correspondence is overlooked as a result.

Broadly generalized, gauge/gravity correspondence tells us that quantum physics and gravity physics are two ways of looking at, describing and understanding the very same thing. If there is a larger lesson to be learned from this insight, it is that holographic/physical or spiritual/material realities are one and the same, and that holographic/physical or spiritual/material ways of looking at the world are just different perspectives on the very same thing. Some problems are impossible to solve from a physical or logical perspective, but are easy to solve from a holographic or spiritual perspective, and vice versa. Truly understanding life, the universe and finding solutions to life's biggest questions and problems may require the ability to seamlessly switch back and forth between these perspectives.

Research related to holonomic brain theory continues to the present day, though the theory remains a largely ignored, but important part of our understanding of the brain. Physicists and another brave medical doctor have, however, evolved holonomic brain theory into quantum mind theories. The physician-physicist team now leading the charge towards a comprehensive, experimentally verifiable quantum mind theory is comprised of Stuart Hameroff, anesthesiologist at the University of Arizona, and Sir Roger Penrose, emeritus professor of mathematics at Oxford University.

In his first book on consciousness, *The Emperor's New Mind,* Penrose, who has made significant contributions to relativity theory and cosmology, outlined a mathematical proof that a computational neural network, which the human brain is conventionally thought to be, cannot give rise to the observed intelligence and complexity of the human mind. The idea is that, if the brain is a computational machine, then we would walk around more like zombies on autopilot, following set programming rather than being able to make meaningfully considered, creative choices about our lives.[11] Penrose proposed that non-computational quantum processes are the only possible explanation for human intelligence. Penrose, however, lacked a detailed proposal for how quantum processes could take place in the brain. Hameroff, who was also researching how quantum processes in the brain could be responsible for consciousness, provided the detailed anatomical structure: cellular microtubules.

Single-cell organisms like bacteria display amazingly intelligent behavior. They respond to environmental changes with incredibly complex solutions and work cooperatively en masse to do so. Single-celled organisms, like amoebae, hunt for food, find mates, learn and remember in complex situations, and have even been observed to navigate mazes for food. The intelligent behavior of microorganisms is hard to explain if you believe that brains give rise to intelligence, as single-cell organisms lack both nervous systems and brains. As early as 1957, neurophysiologist and bacteriologist Charles Sherrington proposed that the interior scaffolding of cells, the cytoskeleton, which is primarily made of microtubules, might serve as a sort of nervous system. Microtubules are present in all living cells (except plants cells, which have cell walls instead) and self-assemble to establish cell shape, direct growth and organize cellular functions.

Microtubules are particularly prevalent and stable in nerve cells. In the human body, neurons each contain around a billion microtubules that can reach up to a meter in length. Anesthesia molecules, which temporarily blot out consciousness, as well as the proteins thought to cause Alzheimer's disease, bind to microtubules within brain cells, so microtubules seem to play an important role in human consciousness as well as microbial intelligence.

Microtubules are primarily made of a protein molecule called tubulin. Tubulin is a very interesting protein because it can hold information in a number of ways: it can take on up to twelve different shapes, attach to and be modified by other proteins (MAPS or microtubule-associated proteins) and it is magnetically dipolar. Tubulin molecules are microscopic 'on-off' switches much like transistors, the fundamental building blocks of computers. Tubulin molecules self-assemble into microtubules in very specific patterns, and in nerve cells, tubulin molecules line up dipole to dipole in hexagonal lattices forming networks suitable for information storage and processing.

In the mid-1990s, Penrose and Hameroff proposed that human consciousness is the result of biologically orchestrated, coherent quantum processes in collections of microtubules within brain cells. Their proposal connects consciousness and brain biology to a novel interpretation of quantum physics, which in turn is based on gravity and general relativity – a first step towards a true theory of everything that describes biology and consciousness as well as gravity and quantum fields. In Penrose and Hameroff's *orchestrated objective reduction* or *Orch OR* theory, superposed matter-waves are real and matter can exist in many places at once. Superposed matter creates different geometries in space-time as it spreads out to take different paths through space-time. At a critical point, the energy difference between different space-time geometries becomes too great, and matter-waves collapse out of superposition into single particles in unique positions in space and time.

Large objects can't exist in superposition because the resultant energy difference between space-time geometries would be very large. Quantum particles, however, can exist in superposition for indefinite lengths of time. Moments of *proto-consciousness*, an inherent level of consciousness that exists throughout the universe, occur each time a matter-wave collapses from superposition back into a single particle state. The collapse, or reduction, of matter-waves into particles is objectively determined by the nature of gravity and space-time rather than by an observation or a choice between multiple universes. The brain utilizes this objective reduction threshold to create cyclical, sustained states of superposition where multiple electrons become entangled with one another across tens of thousands of microtubules. Reduction of the superposed electron-waves back into electron particles is biologically orchestrated by nerve cells in the brain to produce consciousness.

In the brain, superposition occurs across entire regions of the brain, and consciousness literally "moves around the brain in a mobile synchronized zone, within which isolated, entangled microtubules carry out quantum computations and orchestrated objective reduction."[12] Each cycle of superposition is imbued with cognitive information, such that integration, non-computational information processing and moments of consciousness can occur. These cyclical moments of meaningful, cognitive awareness and choice are fed back through microtubules, which, coupled to neuronal activity, allow causal control over behavior and neural plasticity (the reorganization or rewiring of neuronal pathways). Human consciousness occurs in discrete moments, that occur between 30 and 75 times per second, arising from the brain's overall beat frequency – the combination and interference of multiple higher frequency microtubule vibrations within the brain – in line with EEG measurements, the 'flickering' of consciousness trained meditators report and the number of thoughts per second yogic and Buddhist texts report we have.

Orch OR was harshly criticized when it was introduced,

mostly because the brain was thought to be "too warm, wet and noisy" for the delicate quantum coherence proposed by the theory to take place. The theory has, however, stood the test of time and has led to novel research that, so far, supports the predictions made by the theory. In 2006 quantum coherence, where electrons spread out in superposition across multiple cells, was confirmed to occur in plants and is now thought to be an essential to photosynthesis. Warm quantum coherence has also been found to play an essential role in bird-brain navigation, the sense of smell, the folding of DNA and proteins, and water in living cells. In 2013, Japanese researchers confirmed that quantum effects do occur in microtubules at body temperature, and that microtubules, normally extremely good insulators, become exceedingly good conductors at certain resonant frequencies of applied alternating current.[13]

Penrose and Hameroff suggest that their theory is not complete, and a more complete theory is likely to be far more complex, but that by formulating a testable, falsifiable theory that has so far stood up to experimental investigation, they have firmly brought the study of consciousness into the realm of respectable scientific investigation. In doing so, they have started to further ease the 'Copenhagen taboo' on making inferences about the human mind based on quantum physics.

What I find most interesting about Penrose and Hameroff's work is that it points to several levels of mind with a sharp distinction between mind as a neural network and mind as a quantum process that yields both consciousness and non-computable information processing. On one level, the brain clearly functions as the reasoning, learning pattern recognizing neural network that medicine and science have a substantial understanding of. Underneath the neural activity we can see and measure, however, there appears to be four or more levels of self-similar activity and structure. Underneath and giving rise to all of it are microtubule networks, which, by utilizing quantum superposition to process information, offer an exponential increase in the theoretical processing power of the brain: a true quantum leap in intelligence. Hameroff and Penrose calculate the processing power of tubulin networks within a single neuron to be ten quadrillion (10^{16} or one thousand trillion) operations per second. Conventional approaches that calculate the processing power of the brain based only on the number of connections between neurons give the same number for the entire human brain! We may be a quadrillion times smarter than science once thought we were, and artificial intelligence may be a lot further off than many scientists once hoped (or feared).[14]

Quantum information processing is particularly suited to problems where the best solution out of many possibilities must be found. Using superposition, quantum computers (which are in their infancy) are able to compare many solutions to a problem simultaneously, whereas ordinary serial processing computers must generate one answer to a problem at a time, then compare each answer to every other answer. Deceptively simple problems like finding the fastest route around a city when there are many stops to make are very, very hard to solve by calculating one solution at a time because the number of solutions multiplies exponentially with the number of stops. Ordinary serial computers can take hours to generate and compare the millions of possible solutions to such seemingly simple problems. Deceptively simple problems like finding the minimum number of people to invite to a party so that a certain number of guests know each other and a certain number don't are considered realistically impossible to solve computationally by mathematicians if 6 or more guests of each type are to be invited to a party. By generating and comparing all answers to such problems simultaneously, quantum processing can quickly solve these types of optimization problems that are considered computationally unsolvable.

If the human mind does have two interacting components, a

serial logic like component and quantum like component, the quantum mind would be naturally better at solving problems typical of the human condition, like "What should I do now?". In any given moment, every human being on the planet has nearly infinite options to choose from. We can turn left or right, walk or sit, work or play, sleep or eat, rest or adventure, socialize or meditate, etc. Among each of these choices, we have nearly infinite options: what to eat, who to play with, how to work, etc. Choosing the best solutions from amongst infinite possibilities is one way to characterize the human condition and it should be no surprise that part of our mind is perfectly and exquisitely designed to do so.

The fact that following one's heart, gut and intuition in life works out far better than decisions based on logic alone (in my experience at least) should also not be surprising. If part of our mind, the part that isn't 'in' our brains, is able to instantly select the best solutions out of millions of possibilities, as a quantum bio-computer might be capable of, then what we have labeled intuition is simply part of our mind doing what it does naturally rather than a mystical ability. Intuition then can be understood simply as a very complex form of thought, a form of thought that is far superior to logic for making decisions when there are many variables or possibilities involved.

If we can accept that the quantum like component of our mind exists in a second, information-based, holographic like level of reality, then intuition and our quantum minds deserve a whole new level of appreciation. If our quantum minds are informed by the actual state of the universe, past, present and future, then our thoughts are not solely the imaginary constructs of our brains. Our quantum minds would be inherently telepathic and would be capable of solving problems by integrating a staggering breadth of actual information about the state of our environment, the future, and other quantum minds. Pure intuition would not be just a good guess. Pure intuition would represent a calculated optimization solution based on direct real time information, including information about the future.

'Thinking' solely within our quantum minds would not be imaginary or conceptual; rather, it would represent very real optimization solutions based on *all* relevant, real information – a staggering level of genius that is difficult to appreciate. Connected to and integrated with neural networks in our brains, however, what we might call our *bio-minds*, our quantum minds would not only reflect actual information about the state of the universe. Each cycle of quantum information processing would be imbued with cognitive information from our bio-minds: information obtained through our physical senses, from our memories, and/or imagined information along with a desire, question, and intention.

The thinking of an integrated bio/quantum mind would likely be mixed: partly based on real information reflecting the actual state of the universe, and partly imaginary, based on the bio-mind's conceptual or made-up information. However, if we could quiet our bio-minds so that no imaginary or false information is imbued in each cycle of quantum information processing, accurate information about the state of the rest of the universe, past, present or future could be obtained.

Optimization solutions generated by a quantum mind with access to information about past, present and future states of the universe would be infallible, and would represent a staggering level of inclusive genius, if a quantum mind could be imbued with 'pure' or 'clean' cognitive information in the form of a question or intention, and the answer understood. I believe this is exactly what skilled telepaths, shamans, gurus and spiritual luminaries are able to do to obtain accurate information and 'wisdom' about any decision, problem, or subject, past, present or future.

I also believe that when we purposefully wonder about a life choice, decision or topic, then let go and relax into a receptive state, we *imbue our quantum minds with cognitive information.* Our quantum minds, which I believe are a component or part of our connected minds, then integrate a staggering breadth of information related to the subject we wondered about and return 'optimization solutions'. Optimization solutions come back to us in the form of *sentience*: amalgams of sensory information, feelings, ideas, emotions, awareness and knowings. I believe that during this process, our connected minds explore near infinite numbers of optimization solutions, in the form of possible futures, simultaneously, using actual information about the state of the world, other minds, and the future. I also believe that telepathic communication between beings occurs through the same sort of process where information and optimization solutions, in the form of 'bubbles' of sentience, are swapped back and forth between beings.

Imbuing one's quantum mind with a universally beneficent intention such as "for my highest good, and the highest good of the planet", as well as a specific question or intention, is therefore highly important and does three things. First, it creates strict parameters around which one's connected mind is asked to explore possible futures and optimization solutions, thereby enabling it to provide better and more specific answers. Secondly, a universally beneficent intention and a specific question vastly narrows down the field of optimization solutions or possible futures to be explored. Solutions to problems, possible futures and life paths that do not support that greater good or have unintended negative consequences are not explored, allowing one's quantum mind to explore much further into the future, and deeper into possibilities that resonate with the highest good. Thirdly, I believe that such universally beneficent intentions invite cooperative, telepathic communication between the connected minds of many beings, who resonate with similar intentions.

In bringing many connected minds together, in alignment

towards a common purpose, I believe that exponentially better, further reaching (into the future and possibility) 'non-computable optimization solutions' are created. The optimization solutions that many connected minds working together would be capable of generating would reflect an astounding level of inclusive genius that finite bio-minds would never be capable of generating, or even appreciating, let alone understanding. This is why, sometimes, when working with pure intention towards desired outcomes and everything goes wrong, we have to trust everything in our lives happens for a reason, for our highest good, even if we can't logically understand in the moment why something is happening to us.

The optimization solutions of many connected minds working together, returned to each being tuned into the process, would serve to guide and inspire every being willing to 'listen' to their connected minds towards the physical manifestation of such solutions. These types of cooperatively generated optimization solutions would become blueprints of sorts around which the actual future would form. If many people consistently tuned into their connected minds with beneficent intention and shared goals, their thoughts and actions would synchronistically unite around the shared vision, allowing many people (and beings) to work together as a telepathically orchestrated whole to realize the shared vision. Many synchronistic occurrences in our own lives, many of humanity's greatest achievements, and many phenomena in nature can best be explained as the result of such telepathically orchestrated co-creation.

The law of attraction, the well-known new age axiom that your thoughts create your reality, and that focusing our thoughts and emotions with sensory detail manifests resonant experiences into our lives, can be understood as telepathically orchestrated co-creation. Understanding that the law of attraction functions through telepathic co-creation rather than through a mysterious, sometimes beneficent, sometimes indifferent universe goes a long way in explaining many of the common successes and failures working with the law of attraction, and allows those practicing the art of manifestation to do so with greater precision and success.

Our entire universe has in fact always functioned through telepathic co-creation, continually evolving in cyclic loops around collective ideas and memories that guide, inspire and drive the behavior and function of everything, living or not. These collective ideas and memories have functioned perfectly for billions of years to create the universe we see now, but as conscious beings, we now have the ability to recognize the collective ideas and memories that drive us, let go of what no longer serves us, and skillfully contribute to the creation and manifestation of new collective ideas that serve, fulfill and thrill us.

We will explore the hypothesis of morphic resonance, the scientific term for telepathic co-creation, in later chapters. For now, simply notice that everything in nature and our lives has a pattern. Sometimes these patterns are simple, cyclic, or geometric, often they are fractal and complex, and difficult to discern. But at the core of every pattern, there is a formative recipe that exists outside of space and time. When you perceive these recipes, you understand nature and yourself.

Now, this whole two minds conjecture may seem like a stretch, except that for decades, cognitive psychologists have described the human mind as being comprised of two systems. *System 1* (the label widely used in psychology) is very fast, operates effortlessly, automatically and near instantaneously with little sense of voluntary control, so we don't generally even realize we are using it. It is nonverbal, associative and abstract, and is thought to process massive amounts of information simultaneously. We use system 1 to do complex tasks like move our bodies, manipulate objects, understand sounds and recognize or compare objects and faces. System 1 is intuitive, sensory, emotional and works so quickly, with such complexity, that we can't watch or understand how it works. Most people have no conscious awareness when they are using system 1, or that they even have a system 1. It is the metaphorical water in which we swim. System 1 has therefore been labeled our unconscious mind.

System 2 on the other hand is slow. We can follow it working, so we are aware of and understand its functioning. System 2 requires concentration and effort to use. It works sequentially, one step at a time. It focuses attention, logically solves problems and makes decisions. System 2 is what most people think of as 'themselves' because we can watch it working (thinking). We can explain 'what we were thinking' when we use system 2, so system 2 has been labeled the conscious mind.

The two systems of thought that psychologists broadly recognize all humans use bear an uncanny resemblance to the quantum mind/bio-mind system that quantum mind theories point to. System 2, what psychologists label our conscious mind, has the qualities of a computational neural network. The conscious mind is relatively easy to study. We can observe our conscious minds working and explain 'what we were thinking', so the conscious mind has been studied ad nauseam by psychologists and psychiatrists and is relatively well understood.

The unconscious mind is, however, an enduring mystery to science and medicine that defies material explanation. Scientifically documented abilities attributed to the unconscious mind include:

- photographic memory
- recognition of messages displayed too quickly or spoken too softly to be detected consciously
- the ability to accurately count hundreds of objects instantaneously
- the ability to count seconds into the tens of thousands

- the ability to solve complex math problems instantaneously
- production of stigmata and other wounds
- the ability to painlessly and bloodlessly sustain wounds and impalements through skin and muscle
- changes in eye color, changes in body shape, changes in allergies (particularly in transitions between personalities in cases of schizophrenia)
- spontaneous healing of 'incurable' conditions
- precognition, clairvoyance, spontaneous knowing
- various forms of telepathy
- et cetera

All of these abilities are impossible for a neural network isolated in our brains to perform or orchestrate. However, if part of our minds is not in our brains at all, but resides in a second level of reality, a holographic, information-based level of reality that gives rise to physical reality, then many of these so-called paranormal abilities are understandable and very normal. There is nothing paranormal about them. The astounding feats our so-called unconscious minds are capable of are simply the result of informed quantum information processing.

Magical and paranormal phenomena, such as spontaneous healing, are the result of changes to information structures in the second level of reality that gives rise to physical reality, and therefore our physical bodies. Holographic information, existing in a non-local, second reality, expressing itself into three-dimensional physical reality is simply the basis of how everything in our world is created and functions. The mind can then be thought of as an intermediary, or a bridge between these two realities, and a tool through which holographic information expresses, perceives and understands itself.

If system 1 does indeed correspond to a quantum like mind, existing in a second, information-based level of reality that gives rise to the physical world, then labelling system 1 our unconscious mind is, however, as deeply unfortunate as it is untrue. Untrue because if system 1 is a quantum mind, then it is our true conscious mind: it is how and where each and every moment of conscious awareness we experience occurs. Unfortunate, because this part of our minds may be orders of magnitude more intelligent than our logical, thinking minds and infinitely more capable of understanding anything we desire to know about.

By labelling this part of our minds our 'unconscious', we have collectively mislabeled, misunderstood, disparaged, denied and vastly underutilized the most intelligent part of ourselves and the source of our consciousness. If we do indeed have quantum like minds that can perform infinitely complex optimization calculations using actual information about the state of the universe, then it is our quantum minds, not our thinking minds, that represent the possibility of true consciousness – full, accurate and timely awareness of ourselves, our infinite potentials, our place in the universe, and all of the effects of our choices and actions.

The Synergetic Effect

I cannot be contained because I'm the container. You can't contain the container, man! You can't contain the container! I used to believe that who I was ended at the edge of my skin, that I had been given this little vehicle called a body from which to experience creation, and though I couldn't have asked for a sportier model, it was after all a loaner and would have to be returned. Then, I learned that everything outside the vehicle was a part of me, too, and now I drive a convertible. Top down, wind in my hair!

~ Jim Carrey, MUM Graduation Speech, May 24, 2014

The idea that consciousness and information exist in the universe in a second, nonphysical level of reality and that this second level of reality pervades and influences all physical space and matter may still seem nonsensical and ridiculous. The fact that our minds actually exist in a second, nonphysical level of reality, where they interact with the wider world, and have access to all kinds of interesting and useful information, can evoke outright existential terror. Even if we can convince ourselves that our consciousness isn't the product of our brains, and will survive the demise of our physical body, second realities, death and our connected minds may still seem like the great unknown: uncomfortable subjects to contemplate that don't have anything to do with our day-to-day lives.

If we can get past our discomfort, and can begin to embrace the idea that our consciousness is non-locally spread out across the universe, and constantly interacts with our brains, bodies and the world around us, we can begin to notice how often, and how profoundly, telepathic interactions affect our everyday lives. Once we get comfortable with the expanse and interactive nature of our consciousness, we can start to free our consciousness from the confines of our brains, and experience the world in entirely new ways. In doing so, we can also become accountable for our telepathic influence on the world around us. We can *really* become conscious, understand just how powerful beyond measure we really are, and we can begin to consciously co-create our own lives.

Clues as to how our minds are spread over the universe and interact with the material world around us can be found in experiments conducted at Princeton University over a span of 30 years. In the 1970s, a small group of engineers at Princeton began to fear that if human consciousness could affect machines or electronics, then the increasingly delicate complexity of machinery, and the proliferation of electronic control systems in everything from airplanes to nuclear power plants, could put people at enormous risk. If human thought or emotion could influence machinery or electronics, even slightly, then human thought could also cause critical malfunctions and disastrous losses of life and property, if safeguards were not engineered into machines and electronics.

Starting in 1979, the Princeton Engineering Anomalies Research (PEAR) program conducted experiments designed to measure the degree to which human consciousness affects matter, machines and electronics, if at all. The aim of the program was to learn what, if any, safeguards need to be engineered into technology to prevent malfunction due to the influence of human consciousness, not to prove anything per se. The experiments, however, yielded some profound insights into the nature of consciousness-matter interactions.

The PEAR experiments documented mind-machine influences in every kind of machine and electronic device tested, including mechanical, electronic, optical, acoustical and fluid devices. Human subjects (referred to as operators) tried to use only their minds to influence machines, trying to do things like get:

- a carefully monitored pendulum to swing more to one side than another
- a fountain to spurt more to one side than another
- 9,000 balls to fall into slots, more towards one side of a pegged track than another

Most of the studies used electronic random binary number generators, machines that randomly spit out strings of 0s or 1s. Operators tried to influence the output of the machines, without physically touching the machines at all, to produce more 1s, or more 0s, using only their thoughts.

PEAR researchers determined that, left alone, the random number generators produced strings of strictly random numbers, as expected. However, when focused on by an operator, the machines consistently produced results that were skewed from the expected random output. Over millions of trials, on average, operators were able to influence the random number generators to produce one extra 1 or 0, once out of every 10,000 1s or 0s generated, a 0.0001% average influence. Though the effect was small, it was observed across every type of system studied, over millions of trials, and the effect was very significant. The statistical certainty that the observed influence was genuine, and not random, was a trillion to one.[15]

If you believe in science and statistics as methodologies for exploring and understanding the natural world, then the PEAR results constitute very significant scientific evidence that our minds influence matter at a distance (and therefore cannot be isolated in our brains). Coupled with the knowledge that quantum physics tells us that there is an inherent level of uncertainty in the movement and interactions of all matter, a tiny window of influence through which the consciousness of an observer might exert an influence, the idea that consciousness influences and interacts with matter is hard to dismiss. What is more interesting than the mind-matter influence itself is what this influence at a distance tells us about ourselves. The important thing to understand about the PEAR experiments is that there was no physical contact, energy transfer or detectable signal whatsoever between operators and machines, and the mind-matter effects were observed independent of distance and time.

Experiments where target machines and operators were separated by distances of thousands of miles yielded the same results as experiments where operators and machines were placed in the same room. Even experiments where operators tried to influence machines hours before, or hours after, the machines spit out their strings of numbers showed the same mind-matter influence. If there was an undetected electromagnetic signal or energy transfer between operator and machine, the effects would have decreased with distance, and certainly would not have occurred when operators and machines were separated by thousands of miles, or in time.

There was no possible way a mediating signal, or energy transfer, could have occurred between operators and machines. The observed mind-matter influences had to be the result of changes *inside* target machines – changes caused by operators' minds – not an outside influence acting on the machine. Without an energy transfer, there could not be a force to push or pull the workings of a machine in a particular direction. Somehow, operators' minds had to be getting inside target machines. The question is, how could a person's mind possibly find and get inside a machine, especially machines that are thousands of miles away? How could someone's mind possibly understand, let alone change the inner workings of electronics, let alone fountains, pendulums or thousands of cascading balls? What sort of changes could operators' minds possibly cause?

The most straightforward explanation is this: people's minds don't *get* inside electronics, machines, and matter. Our minds are *already* inside machines and matter, and we are influencing everything around us, machines included, all the time. Part of our minds is already in everything, all the time. We are always influencing everything around us, all the time, even if we aren't consciously aware we are doing it. When we focus on a machine, or anything for that matter, the effect, what I call the *synergetic effect*, becomes more pronounced, and statistically detectable.

The conclusion that part of our minds is in everything readily explains how telepathy works: we can obtain information about anything we focus on because, when we focus on something, we bring consciousness to the part of our minds that is already part of whatever we focus on. It's possible to obtain 'inside out' telepathic information about anything we want to know about because part of our mind is already inside anything we choose to focus on. Focus allows us to separate out a portion of our telepathic experience of the world, to go from being 'one with everything' to 'one with a specific part of everything'.

Most of the time, our synergetic influence on the world, and the world's synergetic influence on us, is so subtle it's impossible to notice. Sometimes, however, synergetic effects are very noticeable and we don't need to resort to physics or spiritual teachings to understand that our consciousness is non-local, and that part of our minds is in everything around us. All we need to do is stop dismissing our experiences of the world that don't match logical materialist beliefs about how the world 'should' work for a few moments and notice how the world does work. If we simply consider our own life experiences, most of us will quickly and inevitably notice that we are being affected by everything around us all the time, and also that we affect everything around us all the time. We may in fact already be so familiar with the effects of our minds in everything around us that we have a name for the effect: luck. Most of us assume, or insist, that luck is random, but haven't really taken the time to notice just how much people's state of mind affects the seemingly random events of their lives.

We have all probably had days when everything that could possibly go wrong, against all odds, does, and hopefully days when everything that could go right, goes right. You may even have had days when every piece of electronics you touch malfunctions, you hit every red light, you spill any liquid you walk near, and every interaction you have goes sideways through no discernible fault of your own. If you have, you've probably noticed that when things go wrong, they tend to go wrong all at once, when you're in a rush, really stressed out, or angry.

Murphy's law, the adage that if something can go wrong it will, is labeled a law for a reason. Murphy's law, in my experience, applies more on certain days than others, usually on high stress, critical life outcome days, as well as around certain people more than others. In my experience, there is an uncanny and direct correlation between the state of a person's mind and their luck, on any given day, as well as in life in general. You may know people who are somehow capable of breaking everything they even walk by, who create literal chaos wherever they go, just by virtue of their presence. You may even know someone whom bad luck seems to follow, who always has a story to tell, around whom seemingly random chaotic events consistently happen.

You might know someone who gets dumped on at every turn; who manages to attract every injustice in life. I know people who are so entrenched in being victims, who have attracted so much persecution and bad luck, that they have literally been punched in the face by a random stranger while walking down the street, completely minding their own business. You may also know people who brighten every room they enter, who experience luck and happiness at every turn on their life's path. The luckiest people I know, who constantly win contests, money at the casino and have things gifted to them randomly, are also the people who already feel that they have everything. Lack and struggle don't enter their minds, or their experience of the world, ever. The world consistently reflects their coherent, grounded, abundant, life-loving mindsets back to them. Luck is simply the world around us reflecting our thoughts and state of mind back to us, because our mind is in everything around us, all the time.

My own brother is an entertaining example of the effect one's state of mind has on their surroundings. Over the course of a few years, my brother's job became more and more stressful. He moved an entire manufacturing operation to China and had to fly between opposing time zones biweekly for several years. During that time, he suddenly began getting stung or bitten by every kind of insect and sea creature imaginable, every time he ventured out into nature, whether it was on a beach in Mexico or in his own backyard. He was the preferred meal for mosquitoes and has been stung by bees, wasps, and jellyfish, bitten by a black widow spider and who knows what else, in some very sensitive places, every year for over half a decade. The frequency with which stinging creatures were able to get into my brother's shorts, and other sensitive places, was almost as strange as the frequency with which he got stung. Days after I wrote this very paragraph, I was treated to a Facebook post of my brother's swollen face, his upper lip swollen to triple its size, the result of bee stings, inside his mouth. Bees, it seems, like energy drinks as much as my brother.

The strange thing about my brother's bites and stings was that the people who were with him didn't seem to get stung or bitten. To make matters worse, my brother inevitably had a worse than average reaction to bites and stings. Simple mosquito bites, for example, looked far worse on him than anyone else, swelling up to three or four times their usual size. We joked that my brother was so stressed out that he stressed out nature and caused her to attack, or that he saw himself as separate from nature, so nature naturally rejected him. We are only half-joking. To me, my brother's bad luck was so uncanny, and his stress and jet lag so apparent, it was clear that nature was simply reflecting his state of mind back to him – because part of his mind, his connected mind, was in everything around him, including insects, who, feeling his stress, became stressed enough themselves to feel the need to defend themselves against him.

Of course, it may still seem like we are jumping to conclusions and making a big deal out of nothing. A trillion to one statistical inference that the human mind can influence matter at a distance might be compelling, but the average 0.0001% influence the PEAR experiments concluded that intentional human thought has on the randomness of random binary systems may seem utterly insignificant, too small to ever possibly make a difference. Even if we do generalize, and make the admittedly giant leap in logic that our minds are in and influencing everything around us, all the time, and assume that all thought influences the world at the same level as found in the PEAR experiments, how significant could a 0.0001% influence in randomness possibly be? What difference could a 0.0001% influence on the randomness of the physical world possibly make? What does this tiny influence tell us about ourselves, our minds, and how we fit into and interact with the physical world? Could such a small influence ever make a difference and why would, in my brother's case, insects seem to be so susceptible to such a small influence?

Under most circumstances the simple objects we deal with in our day to day lives like forks, sticks, stones, cars and billiard balls respond to force, gravity, electricity and chemistry in predictable ways, and follow linear rules where a tiny change, on the order of 0.0001%, doesn't make any difference at all. Throw a rock into the air, swing a pendulum, or roll a ball down the hill, and you can predict exactly what will happen. Tiny deviations in the way you throw the rock or swing a pendulum won't make a difference. However, try landing a rock on the moon – say, by propelling it with a rocket – then an infinitely small deviation can mean the difference between hitting the moon, or missing it altogether.

Similarly, any time substances and objects are put together to interact as a system, circumstances arise very quickly where an infinitely small influence can change everything. Such systems are referred to as nonlinear, or chaotic systems, and are found everywhere. For example, a single pendulum is a linear system, and completely predictable. Put two pendulums together, however, and the system becomes chaotic. Infinitely small differences in where or how a double pendulum is initially released can result in the double pendulum swinging along vastly different paths. Even though simple systems like double pendulums follow simple linear rules of physics, such systems are so sensitive to initial conditions that infinitely small differences in initial conditions can translate into vastly different behaviors and outcomes.

The sensitivity of chaotic systems to infinitely small influences is often referred to as the butterfly effect. Chaos theorists tell us that the tiny breeze created by a butterfly flapping its wings in Tokyo can cause a hurricane in the Atlantic since weather is a chaotic system. If the butterfly flaps its wings in just the right way, at just the right place and time, huge effects can come from very subtle causes. Although many separate objects in our world follow linear rules, nothing in the world is truly separate – our entire planet is, at some level, an interconnected system; one that can become chaotic and nonlinear very quickly. Far from being the exception, circumstances where an infinitely small influence can cascade into massive change can be found everywhere. Moreover, many things in the physical world that appear stable and straightforward are actually highly susceptible to tiny influences, even the ground we walk on.

The physical world actually tends to self-organize into critical states – states where a small influence can cascade into massive and sweeping changes. A simple sand pile is one example of a self-organizing critical state system. A sand pile built by dropping one grain of sand at a time onto the same spot will eventually grow too high and avalanches will occur. How high the sand pile will grow, which grain of sand will trigger an avalanche, how big the avalanche will be, and how it will change the sand pile is impossible to predict. The way in which grains of sand fit together in a growing pile, along with the networks of contacts between sand grains that distribute forces throughout the entire sand pile, are so complex that minute differences in the way any one grain of sand hits the sand pile can mean the difference between no avalanche, a small avalanche, or a sand pile wide avalanche.

Chaotic systems and self-organizing criticality are everywhere, at every level in our universe, from the microscopic structures of water and living cells, to the macroscopic structures and growth of ecosystems, rivers, mountains, tectonic plates and galaxies. The human world is not exempt as stock markets, traffic jams and many parts of our bodies, including our brains, display self-organizing criticality and chaotic, nonlinear behaviors. Even phenomena such as forest fires, the spread of viruses, population growth and evolution follow patterns of self-organizing criticality. Chaos and criticality, circumstances and systems where a 0.0001% influence can have profound effects are everywhere, at every level in our universe, and are the rule, not the exception. I do, however, prefer to use the term *synergetic* over chaotic and critical.

Unfortunately, if we say that the basic nature of the physical world is chaos and criticality, our understanding of the natural world may again be warped by word baggage. Chaos and criticality are both words with negative connotations, and their actual meanings oppose their literal meanings. To say that the world is chaotic in the literal sense suggests that the world defies order and is dangerously unpredictable, whereas in the mathematical sense, chaos implies that there is a beautiful deeper order to what only seems like an unpredictable and random world; a deeper order that can be understood and at least appreciated if not harnessed.

Criticality, in our world, implies crisis, and although crisis events like earthquakes and hurricanes follow patterns of self-organizing criticality, much of the peaceful beauty we see in the natural world, from the shapes of mountains, to rivers, to clouds and galaxies, even our bodies, is the result of self-organizing criticality. So chaos and criticality, in my books, are ironic misnomers. I use the term *synergetic*, meaning elements working together as a whole such that a tiny change in any one part can profoundly affect the whole. It's a far better word to describe the basic nature of our world.

The words we use to describe and understand the nature of our world aren't the point though. The point is to understand the nature we are trying to describe. So if we understand that the basic nature of our world is synergetic, and situations where infinitely small influences can trigger massive changes abound, then the 0.0001% average influence of human thought is very significant, and there are an infinite number of phenomena, circumstances and points in space and time – what we might call *synergetic leverage points* – where a tiny deviation in randomness caused by human thought could influence and cause very large effects in the gross physical world.

So, if part of our mind is in everything we observe, we are always influencing the physical world around us, all the time, because a small part of us is mixed up in everything we observe. If much of the world we observe is synergetically sensitive, complex and delicate enough to amplify small changes from our own consciousness, then our thoughts and consciousness literally change the world around us. In general, the more intricate and complex the systems and beings around us are, the more sensitive they will be to the synergetic effect of our consciousness on them, and the larger the effects will be. Electronics, machinery, insects, animals and people, all very complex systems, will therefore be sensitive to synergetic effects of consciousness. Interacting groups of people, electronics and/or animals even more so. Although the exact effects of one person's consciousness on the world around them can be unpredictable and difficult to control, the general direction and flavor of one's synergetic effect is predictable and controllable. We are responsible for our state of mind, and its effect on the world around us.

In the simplest terms, people's energy, their synergetic effect on the world around them, is either coherent, causing less randomness, or dissonant, causing more randomness. Calmness, connection, ease and flow tend to result from coherence, whereas strife, crisis and calamity tend to result from dissonant energy. Of course a little chaos channeled in the right direction can make life much more entertaining and interesting, and is sometimes needed to keep things from getting static and stale.

We can control our synergetic effect, our synergy with the world, or lack of it, by managing our state through our focus, intention, breathing and spiritual practice. If we are stressed out, judgmental, and unwell, the world around us feels it and reflects our state of mind back to us. The worse you feel, the more dissonant your energy, the more calamity, catastrophe and persecution you create and experience. The more calamity and persecution you create and experience, the more badly you feel, et cetera, et cetera. For anyone with very dissonant energy, who is unaware of their synergetic effect on the world, who is caught in the downward spiral known as *the victim trap,* it seems like the world is against them, they just can't win, that they are cursed, or that they are being punished. They will experience rejection, accidents, disappointment and outright persecution at every turn, becoming more and more beaten down, desperate, untrusting and dissonant with each new negative experience.

The only escape from the victim trap is accepting responsibility for everything that has befallen you, and moving into the role of intentional creator. The upside for anyone who has been caught in the victim trap is that if one's negative experiences can be embraced as personal and undeniable evidence of one's power to attract, create and manifest experience, then accepting one's power and moving into the role of powerful creator is easy.

For those of us who can cultivate coherent energy, who can manage to stay calm, out of judgement, and maintain a loving presence through spiritual practice or pure and authentic positivity, the world can be a magical place. People want to be around energetically coherent people for no reason, connect with them, play in the moment, and seemingly random life events inevitably have a delightful spin: we synchronistically meet new friends who happen to have needed connections, knowledge or information at just the right time; we joyously run into old friends in strange places against all odds; we stumble upon a party, wedding or event, get invited in and have the time of our lives; we happen to walk by a tree as baby squirrels make their first trip out into the world and climb on us; or strangers give us flowers (yes, all these things have happened to my husband or myself). Business meetings flow smoothly and even clients we meet, who were initially combative or in a bad mood, suddenly soften, smile and want to make our day a little easier and happier. Our coherent energy inspires calmness, cooperation and also brings our attention and guides us towards resonantly delightful people, paths, ideas and experiences.

Understanding the synergetic effect, the whole concept of random luck goes out the window. Unlikely occurrences in people's lives can be understood as synergetic effects, rather than random happenings, and the adage that we create our own good fortune is true on more than one level. When light bulbs blow up when we walk into a room, electronics malfunction, insects attack, dogs bite, animals behave strangely, we get into arguments with other people, these seemingly random occurrences are not random at all, they are a reflection of our energy and state of mind.

By far the most important factor in our lives, I think, is the synergetic fit between us and the people we choose to have in our lives. We can complement one another, energizing and lighting up one another, OR we may clash – making one another anxious, angry, sad or physically sick for no particular reason at all. The presence or absence of any one person, place or animal from one's life or any particular situation can affect things in unexpected and strange ways. Human life is about constantly finding the right mix and fit of people, minds and energies to synergetically come together in delightful win-win-win ways.

How the people in our lives perceive us, and how they affect us synergetically, affects us on a very deep level, making us more, or less, of who we are: healthy or ill, happy or sad, calm or nervous. Do the people around you light you up? Or do they dim you and drag you down? Do they make you more of who you are; more of who you want to be? Inspire and energize you, or drain you? And how do you synergetically affect the people around you? Do you observe people with an open and present curiosity, love and delight, so that they light up? Or does your presence bring judgement, fear or anxiety for others? Important questions to constantly be asking when consciously creating the life you want and the person you want to be. The people you are connected to, that see you daily, very much make you who you are – their perception of you, and their synergetic effect on you, can and does affect you at a very deep level.

You are not at all powerless in synergetic dynamics though. Your focus determines, enhances or lessens people's synergetic effects on you, and your effect on the world around you. You can strengthen positive empowered views of self by focusing more on people who light you up; people who make you feel warm and fuzzy, while forgoing thinking about the people who dull you out, anger, sadden or disempower you. Enhance the synergetic effects you want by spending time and strengthening your connections with people who make you feel good and see you how you want to be seen. Lessen negative synergetic effects by not giving those who bring you down a second thought.

It turns out that we should worry about what people think of us, but only for long enough to figure out people's synergetic effects on us, so that we can choose who to spend time with and focus on, and who not to. Remember, though, that we also telepathically inform the people around us how to feel about us through our feelings and beliefs about ourselves, and how we carry ourselves. Your deepest feelings about yourself will always be reflected by the world and people around you, and you teach people how to treat you through your actions. Cultivating respect, patience and love for oneself is perhaps the most important exercise of all for creating a positive synergistic effect on everyone around you, and the reason why reciting affirmations does work on occasion. Just wanting people to see you positively without seeing yourself positively first then vying or manipulating for attention and appreciation usually has the opposite effect than intended.

The nice thing about having telepathic abilities is that synergetic effects are easily perceptible and predictable. The general state of people's minds is fairly easy to perceive as a telepath, and how people will synergetically fit together, which, I think, is why people often go to psychics for help with their love life, family relationships and life decisions. Psychics in general, I think, tend to be very good at perceiving and predicting synergistic fits. You don't have to be very psychically adept to understand and use synergy in your life though. Most of us can perceive the general state of other people's minds through the synergetic effect they have on us.

When someone focuses on us, or we focus on another person, our consciousnesses mix and merge, at the 0.0001% level, or more if we sustain a mutual focus. When our consciousness mixes with another person's, we can perceive the resulting tiny changes in our body, mood, thoughts and state of mind. In other words, we perceive changes in our being or energy caused by other people's synergetic effects on us. When our skin crawls or we're creeped out by someone staring at us, there's a really good reason for it. The consciousness that is observing us doesn't mix well with ours, and is very much inside us, which is why such experiences feel so invasive or creepy, and we feel like we have to 'shake them off' after. On the flip side, when someone observes us with love, appreciation, respect or desire, we feel the truth of these emotions. We feel it deep, deep down in our being and in our bodies as a warm and tingly feeling, or we feel energized and alive, or both.

Telepathy can be thought of partly as a way of becoming very adept at feeling and discerning the effects others have on your own energy system and consciousness, to the point where you can derive information about the consciousnesses you connect with: if your mind is in everything around you, you can feel everything around you with your mind. By noticing the changes and sensations that occur in your body, feelings and mind when you focus on someone or something, you can obtain useful telepathic or psychic information.

First impressions are a great place to practice telepathy, as they are telepathic exchanges, and function through synergetic effects. Anyone who's had a strong first impression knows what a synergetic impression feels like. Our telepathic perceptions are often dismissed as logical conclusions from physical or subconscious cues like body language or physical appearance. But first impressions aren't just about physical cues and logic at all. Noticing what people feel like with your connected mind and correlating how they feel energetically with how they behave is an excellent place to start practicing telepathy. You can hone your senses and become more sensitive to synergetic effects by spending time focusing on nothing in daily meditation, sort of like calibrating a sensitive scale to zero. Cleansing diets, time in silence and other ascetic practices also make you more sensitive to synergetic effects. Exercise caution and have your own back though, the world some of us have to live and work in daily is not necessarily a pleasant place that you want to bring more sensitivity to. Cultivating a stronger sense of self and telepathic resilience through repeated introspection or one pointed focus on specific intentions, ideas or states of being may be more appropriate practice for many.

In general, people's energy, or state of mind, can be understood through their synergetic impression on your energy, which can be categorized on a few spectrums such as coherent or dissonant, harmonious or chaotic, introverted or extroverted, calming or energizing, lit up or shut down, creative or stoic, survivor mind or connected mind focused, et cetera. Consciously noticing where people fit on such spectrums, and mentally running through a list of such qualities as you notice people's synergetic effect on you can bring some structure and consistency to this practice. If you are going to practice though, be careful – this is where beginners tend to get flaky, far out and weird.

Don't get carried away focusing solely on your telepathic impressions and forgetting about logic and the physical world. Especially don't get upset, frightened or angry with your telepathic impressions, just calmly observe and don't judge – they're just impressions. Certainly don't go telepathically looking for judgements or negativity – you'll find both, and enhancing them with your focus will make your life very unpleasant in the process. Noticing energetic nuances and how they correlate with how people dress, groom themselves, hold themselves, communicate, the lifestyles they live and what they do next in the moment is a first step to developing a subtle sensory vocabulary or an energetic rolodex. When you perceive something new or novel with your connected mind, if you have perceived something similar before, you'll have a reference point to understand how it translates into the physical world.

Understanding a little bit about the synergetic observer effect, the next logical question is: How powerful is it? If part of our minds is in everything around us, can we learn to consciously focus to enhance our synergetic effects? Can we become conscious enough of our connected minds to feel synergetic leverage points where a tiny change induced by our consciousness or thoughts will translate into a large change in the gross physical world? With awareness, intent and skill, how powerfully could we do so? Could human thought mean the difference between sunshine and a hurricane, a tremor or an earthquake, a snowball or an avalanche, sickness or health, or the life or death of a living cell and, in turn, an entire living organism? Can one person's focused thought cause a tumor to shrink or grow, a traffic jam versus clear highways, a functioning Internet versus a network crash? How magical are we, or could we learn to be?

Many reports of paranormal powers and phenomena, well catalogued in books such as *The Future of the Body* by Esalen Institute founder Michael Murphy or the annals of the *Journal for Psychical Research*, suggest that the synergetic effect can be very powerful. Phenomena ranging from shaman controlling the weather, to dowsing, to energy healing, to spontaneous remissions from incurable diseases and other mind-body effects are readily explained as happening through exceptionally coherent or powerful synergetic effects. The real answer to the question of how powerful synergetic effects can be comes in four parts:

- the number of people focusing,
- the skill, ability, or coherence of the people focusing,
- the degree or strength of connection between consciousness and subject(s),
- the power or sensitivity of synergetic leverage points that are focused on.

How strong the effects are depends on the confluence of all four factors. Nuances in the PEAR results, consistent nuances that we think lend considerable credence to the PEAR data, tell us a little bit about these factors and the mechanics and nature of synergetic effects. Individual PEAR operators tended to produce signature data, that is, individuals produced the same results over time, and more importantly across very different types of machines. Whether an operator was trying to get an electronic random number generator to spit out more 1s than 0s, or trying to get a random cascade of 9,000 balls to fall to the left side of a track, their influence tended be the same in scale and character. Women tended to produce larger effects, but men tended to be better at influencing results in desired directions – some operators produced an effect but influenced machines in the opposite direction as was intended. A few operators, deemed skilled operators, could produce much larger effects than average, in desired directions. Pairs of operators working together tended to induce larger influences, especially when the operator pairs felt connected.

Connectedness, the feeling of being connected, or resonance, turned out to be a significant factor in PEAR experiments in a number of ways. Operators who felt comfortable and connected to the machines they were trying to influence tended to produce larger influences. Opposite sex operator pairs, especially emotionally bonded pairs, produced much larger results than same sex operator pairs.[16] Groups of people engaged in emotionally moving activities, especially in intimate or sacred settings, were found to produce large effects, reducing the randomness of the machines, even when the groups were not aware of the presence of the machines.

From my personal experience and understanding of the connected mind, the PEAR results make sense; operators' subjective feelings of connection are more than just feelings, they are a very real measure of an operator's synergetic effect and the degree to which operators' minds are *in* target machines. The same goes in life: feelings of connection and love are more than just subjective impressions, they are actual measures of the degree to which your consciousness or mind is shared with another person, place or thing, and the degree to which you synergetically affect one another.

The fourth part of the synergy equation, the power and sensitivity of synergetic leverage points, we think is the most important part. The more important question is probably not so much how powerfully can we influence synergetic leverage points; the question is: How powerful are synergetic leverage points? What do sensitive or powerful leverage points look like? If human thought does influence random binary systems at a 0.0001% level, at what level of sensitivity to randomness do systems become easily influenceable by human thought? Could we engineer a system to allow our minds to control matter and machines from a distance? Or allow communication with disincarnate minds?

Evidence that analog electronics reached the level of sensitivity required to be influenced by a disincarnate mind some time ago abounds in the form electronic voice phenomenon (EVP); cases of which have been documented worldwide. Gary Schwartz at the University of Arizona is among a handful of researchers who have seriously investigated instrumental transcommunication (IVP) using stringent scientific methodologies and produced some compelling evidence with systems purposely engineered and built to facilitate communication with disincarnate minds. Many people who have worked with computers will have noticed an uncanny correlation between the outlooks, stress and moods of their operators and the frequency and timing of system crashes and other problems: computer technology reached synergetic sensitivity long ago. The real answer to the question of mind-matter interaction though may be right behind our eyes, and disappointing to sci-fi enthusiasts.

Hypothetically, if we were to try and engineer a machine that we could control through the synergetic effect, a machine that might also permit disincarnate minds to interact with the physical world, we might imagine that nonlinear or critical state systems could act as antennas for consciousness that could amplify mind-matter influences at the 0.0001% level into a movement or sound. We might imagine that such a machine would require many interconnected critical state systems, the more the better, since many interconnected antennas would be more sensitive to just one. We might imagine that the more interconnected, complex and delicate the system, the more sensitive it would be to the tiny influences of consciousness.

A system made up of many microscopic elements, suspended in liquid, dynamically interconnecting many microscopic physical, electromagnetic, chemical components might offer the most complexity and sensitivity. The machine would then have to be built or wired so that a small change triggered by a thought would cascade through an amplification system and translate into a movement or sound. A machine that follows just one thought command would be cool, but not much fun, so we would want to engineer our thought sensitive critical state system to be self-restoring or homeostatic, so that it would return to a stable critical state each time it was triggered. That way you could make the machine move or produce sound repeatedly. What would such a machine look like? I suspect it would look a lot like a living cell, or a collection of living cells, or a collection of specialized living cells wired to a body: perhaps a brain on top of a body.

If we simply realize that the most delicate, intricate and complex physical systems on earth are also going to be the most sensitive systems to the synergetic effects of consciousness, then the answer to the question of what does a mind-matter interaction machine look like is all around us in nature and right behind our eyes. Containing billions of interacting molecules and proteins, suspended in a carefully maintained liquid environment, living cells are homeostatic, self-sustaining tiny little bags of intricate, synergetically sensitive complexity where the tiny 0.0001% level influence of consciousness can be magnified over trillions of synergetically sensitive interconnected molecules and proteins into gross, meaningful, material changes. Living cells are the perfect synergetic mind-matter interaction machines.

A networked collection of living cells, the brain is the most complex, delicate and intricate (therefore synergetically sensitive) electromagnetic-chemical-physiological system in the known universe. Containing 86 billion or so neurons, each containing a billion or so microtubule tubulin molecules, all intricately networked in layers of three-dimensional hierarchical structures where many carefully controlled dynamically interacting electrochemical reactions and processes take place, the brain is a vast collection of nonlinear and critical state systems, systems we can easily imagine being sensitive to thought influences at the 0.0001% level. In fact, some neuroscientists have proposed that the brain can only be understood through "nonlinear dynamical systems theory – especially the theories of self-organization and chaos."[17] Wiring our brains to our bodies, our nervous systems are perfect amplification systems to translate the tiny influence of consciousness into movement and sound in the physical world. It seems that the perfect machine for mind-matter interaction already exists in the form of the human brain and body, and I don't think it's a coincidence at all. If our minds are in fact not in our brains, it makes perfect sense that the brain has the exact properties that a mind-matter communication device would need to have given the 0.0001% level of influence observed by PEAR researchers.

So based on this little thought experiment, our brains and bodies are the ultimate channels for consciousness: perfectly and beautifully designed bundles of self-organizing, homeostatic, self-restoring synergetic complexity. Our bodies are specially tuned antennas for consciousness; at multiple levels, we are, in a sense, meat puppets. We are not simply the puppets though, we are not our bodies; we are what moves, animates, shapes and forms our bodies through the synergetic effect. We are not our physical vehicles; we are the drivers, and our own mechanics. We are the consciousness that grows, shapes, maintains, operates and perceives from and through our physical vehicles.

Many of us are at odds with our bodies, deeply uncomfortable in our own skins, as if our bodies are rejecting us, or we are rejecting them. Our bodies are 'out of tune' with our own consciousness, and the life giving, inspiring, enlivening and healing effects of our 'spirits'. For many of us, our souls, spirits, consciousness or connected minds, if you will, no longer freely flow through our bodies to guide, shape and inspire the cells of our bodies and the bodily systems they make up toward symbiosis, health, well-being and vitality. We have collectively tuned out of our connected minds, the tool that permits us to flow and shape the holograph of our minds into beautiful, coherent, perfectly functioning physical forms. We have tuned into the dramas of our survivor minds, and the belief that we are separate, vulnerable and powerless machine-like biological organisms that must be medicated, dissected and stitched into proper functioning.

Tuning back into our own consciousness, fine-tuning the antennas our own bodies and brains back towards sensitivity and receptivity to the profoundly beneficial synergetic effects of our connected minds is not difficult. Many of us are already doing so instinctively, and there are many practices that are specifically designed to do so, as well as places on the planet conducive to this process. When I do yoga, a system designed and developed over millennia to yoke or merge mind, body, spirit and the divine, I often inwardly giggle as I compare poses to fiddling with a rabbit ear antenna on an old TV set; each hatha yoga pose having been developed to focus and tune the body and mind in a particular way toward the merger of individual consciousness with the divine. Practicing yoga, or any movement in nature or sacred spaces, enhances the process and its effects.

Though beneficial, complex practices are not required to tune your body towards your own consciousness. One only needs to unplug from external dramas, and focus on the present moment, on one's own consciousness and body, through movement of any kind, time in nature, or through stillness. Our connected minds are always there, and always on, subtly informing, animating and shaping our bodies all the time; we just have to stop distracting ourselves and resisting. Fueling the body with conscious, living foods rather than dead, synthetic or chemically altered foods is also of great help in this regard. You are what you eat, and we are deeply affected by all matter and consciousness we bring into our bodies.

While our own consciousness, every consciousness we take into our bodies, and everything around us profoundly affect us, we also affect every consciousness around us and connected to us. We especially affect every synergetic leverage point around us, from weather systems, to traffic, to sand piles, to the most sensitive synergetic leverage points of all – other living beings. Mosses, bacteria, mushrooms, trees, insects, cats, dogs, horses, dolphins: we are all in communication with each other, all the time, synergistically affecting one another whether we acknowledge it or not.

From a telepath's perspective, many people's complete refusal to acknowledge their synergetic effect on everyone and everything around them speaks very loudly energetically, both on an individual level, and as a culture. In the West, our predominant focus on competition, stress, worry, judgement and lack in our own tiny bio-minds, and our refusal to acknowledge, co-create or synergize with the living beings around us is a form of communication in itself; one that has consequences. Native

Americans say that only white men get bitten by rattlesnakes because they see themselves as separate from nature – I wholeheartedly agree.

To animals, indigenous peoples and the more sensitive, empathic people among us who live in their connected minds as much as their bio-minds, the average modern human must seem like a giant, blindfolded toddler, belligerent and oblivious to all of the energies and consciousness around them. The consciousness of every other being in the natural world is very much in communication with everything else around them. Most of us are blind to an entire level of existence and being, mostly because we refuse to acknowledge it out of our mistaken belief that we know better; that science knows better. This blind obstinance has consequences, consequences that any environmentalist and many native peoples can tell you about; but beyond the environmental consequences, we are simply missing out big time. The delight, richness and joy of living life on two levels, in two places at once is impossible to put into words. You don't know what you are missing, or how depleted and underutilized you have become, until you let yourself dip your awareness back into what is really the source of your physical being – your connected mind.

What Words Can't Express

The fish trap exists because of the fish; once you've gotten the fish, you can forget the trap. The rabbit snare exists because of the rabbit; once you've gotten the rabbit, you can forget the snare. Words exist because of meaning; once you've gotten the meaning, you can forget the words. Where can I find a man who has forgotten words so I can have a word with him?
~ Chuang Tzu

Over the first few millennia of documented human history, science – the systematic pursuit and sharing of knowledge – mostly concerned itself with inner or spiritual exploration. The oldest sciences are the *inner* sciences. Humans, over the last several millennia, have diligently explored our inner world, and documented what they've found in religious texts of all sorts. In recent centuries, however, scientists fiercely fought to restrict scientific exploration to the study of the material world. Many scientists went so far as to declare matter the fundamental substance of nature, and all phenomena, including consciousness, solely the result of material interactions. Any exploration of non-material mechanisms or phenomena has since been declared unscientific, or irrational, and anything non-physical has been declared nonexistent or imaginary.

As science has heavily influenced the worldview of modern culture, many people now view the world, and themselves, as a complex material machine composed solely of separate, interacting material parts. As a result, many of us dismiss anything that cannot be explained by material interactions as impossible. The reductionist, materialist view of the world that insists that any connection or communication that cannot be explained through the interactions of matter and energy is impossible magic has, however, been disproven repeatedly.

Unfortunately, the scientific proof that we are living in a world that is deeply interconnected in ways that defy material explanation is typically referenced as a mystery, or 'a problem', by mainstream scientists. Most scientists don't like to talk about problems with their work, so we rarely hear about what can be referred to as the *wholeness* or *coherence problem* in science through the mainstream media. The coherence problem turns up in science and life again and again when things that are separated in space and time behave as if they are not separate at all, as if they are in communication with one another, affect one another or seem to work together as if they are a connected, orchestrated whole.

In life, we recognize coherence as synchronicities, serendipity, irony and karma. In cosmology, the coherence problem turns up in a number of places: the amount of matter in the universe, the number of elementary particles, their masses, the universal physical constants such as the speed of light and the gravitational constant are all extraordinarily and improbably finely-tuned to permit the universe we see and the existence of intelligent life. Slight changes in the nature of energy or matter and stable atoms wouldn't form, planets would fly off their orbits, and life could not exist. The physics of our universe, and everything in it, all fit together in just the right way to permit intelligent life, as if the same intelligence that observes the universe also had a part in its creation. The coherence problem in cosmology is so glaring that physicists have actually given it a name: the anthropomorphic principle.

In anthropology, coherence shows up as ideas appearing at the same time in different parts of the world in ancient cultures that could not have been in physical contact with one another. Coherence also shows up in many so-called primitive peoples who display inexplicably advanced knowledge of things such as astrology, architecture, or the medicinal properties of plants. Traditional healers often tell anthropologists that the plants themselves gave them, or their ancestors, knowledge of their healing properties – meaning that, if true, plants and people aren't separate at all, but are in communication with one another, and are working together as a symbiotic whole.

In psychology, coherence shows up in archetypes that appear across many cultures, and as acausality, as defined by psychologist Carl Jung, who proposed the idea of the collective unconscious to account for the coherence he encountered again and again exploring the human psyche. In medicine, coherence between mind and body is labeled the placebo effect, and is so powerful and widely acknowledged that it must be accounted for in every scientific trial of new drugs. Practitioners of holistic medicines harness a wide variety of coherences between mind, body and health to effect cures. Everything from our posture and the alignment of our joints, to minute concentrations of chemicals and plant compounds in our tissues, to the types and varieties of bacteria in our guts, to the flow of energy through our bodies is deeply and profoundly connected to our health and well-being.

In quantum physics, the wholeness problem appears as non-locality and entanglement: the fact that quantum particles – the building blocks of everything in the physical world – can become entangled so that the behavior of one particle instantaneously changes based on what happens to the distant particle it is entangled with. This happens no matter how far apart the two particles are. Entangled particles behave as if they are connected through a 'back door' across space and time, as if they are one thing, two parts of one whole, even though they are separated in space.

In biology the coherence problem shows up in evolution, where the fossil record shows new species appearing and adapting to environmental changes far faster than random mutation should ever permit: for complex organisms, simultaneous changes in DNA at several places within a gene are required to create new, functioning genes, and new species. According to mathematical physicist Fred Hoyle, author of *The Intelligent Universe*, the probability of the complex life forms we see on our planet having evolved by chance, because of random mutations, is about the same as a hurricane blowing through a scrap yard and assembling a functioning airplane.

Hoyle relates creating a functioning gene to solving a Rubik's cube: like the colored squares on a Rubik's cube, the DNA in a functioning gene must be in the correct sequence. So creating a functioning gene is similar to solving a Rubik's cube. If a blind man tried to solve a Rubik's cube by random trial and error alone, making one move every second, it would take 126 billion years for him to work through all the possible moves. The universe is estimated to be 13.8 billion years old, so solving a Rubik's cube or creating a functioning gene through random trial and error is exceedingly unlikely. If gene mutations are blind, and only occur through random trial and error, our planet simply has not been around long enough for complex life to exist. The genetic mutations that facilitate the evolution of life we see on this planet seem to be guided somehow, or spontaneously fine-tuned to the environment, again as if the organisms, their genes and the ecosystems they exist in are a connected, cohesively orchestrated whole.

The coherence problem also shows up in living organisms, at many levels, including in the brain. Pioneering neurophysiologist Benjamin Libet at the University California, San Francisco has shown that our brains become aware of physical sensations on the body before stimuli leading to the sensations occur. Our brains, it seems, 'project' sensations back in time, so that we perceive physical sensations at the same moment physical stimuli reach our bodies, even though nerve impulses take a finite amount of time to travel from the skin to the brain. According to bio-physicists like Mae-Wan Ho, author of *The Rainbow and the Worm: The Physics of Organisms*, the multitude, speed and complexity of the adjustments, changes and responses required to maintain a living organism cannot be explained through biochemical and electromagnetic communication between cells and body parts alone. Every part of living organisms, from the tens of thousands of genes and hundreds of thousands of proteins that make up single cells, to each organ within the bodies of animals, is in continuous and instantaneous communication with every other part. No matter how diverse the parts of living organisms, when functioning correctly, they act in unison, as just one thing, much like an orchestra with an invisible conductor.

Coherence, connection and wholeness are so pervasive and influential in our world, and have shown up so often in scientific investigation that scientists such as Gregg Braden and Rupert Sheldrake, whose work we will talk about later, have referred to the science of coherence and connection as 'new science' and the reductionist, materialist science, widely taught in high schools for decades, as disproven, 'old science'. New science, the science of connection, coherence and wholeness, recognizes that nature has a sort of collective memory, and a purposeful consciousness that permeates all space and time. The new science recognizes that we live in an informed universe where action at a distance, as well as the sharing of information through unmediated connections across time and space, is not only possible, it is the basic nature of the universe and how the world and everything in it functions. We don't hear much about the new science in the mainstream media because much of the scientific community, along with the journalists and public who look to them to understand how the world works, just can't let go of the old materialist worldview, and dismiss much of this new science out of hand.

It's hard to abandon everything you've been taught and believed in all your life. It's instinctual to defend what you know, flaws and all. As such, many of the glaring problems with mainstream materialist scientific views of the world are swept under the rug or only discussed discretely by scientists in non-public forums; problems such as the 'missing heritability problem' in genetics, a problem that is well-known to geneticists, but not the public. The problem is that geneticists, who once thought that genes were primarily responsible for pretty much everything we are and do, have now discovered that individual genes only account for a minority of inherited diseases, behaviors and physical characteristics. All the answers to human nature and health, it turns out, are not in our material genes. These research 'problems' that mainstream science keeps running into rarely make the news, while discoveries that fit within mainstream scientific views often do.

As such, many people are surprised to learn that the scientists who have let go of insisting that the world only works through material means have not only repeatedly confirmed that unmediated connection, or telepathy, occurs in many ways and forms, they have also started to answer many of our burning questions about death and human consciousness. Questions like: "Is there life after death?", "Do we have a soul?" or "Are spirits real?" Such questions are very complex, and carry so many hidden presumptions that intelligent discussion and investigation seems impossible. By asking better questions, and ingeniously devising ways to measure things that were once considered unmeasurable and therefore impossible to investigate scientifically, modern researchers have documented concrete evidence that goes a long way to answering some of life's biggest questions.

In science, just as in life, ask better questions and you get better answers. Better questions like: "Does consciousness survive death?", "Does the mind exist without the body?" and "Can we perceive or interact with nonphysical consciousness?" Such questions don't lend themselves well to study by researchers who have been trained and equipped to investigate physical-material subjects; but just because something can't be measured in a lab or captured on camera doesn't mean it can't be studied scientifically. To study some phenomena, you have to choose methods, sets, settings and subjects very carefully, and maybe get out of the lab and into real world conditions.

With cleverly designed experiments, rigorous methodologies, and careful study of screened mediums in more natural work settings, researchers like Gary Schwartz at the University of Arizona and Julie Beischel at the Windbridge Institute have produced some rather irrefutable evidence that consciousness does survive death, that the mind does persist without the body, and that we can interact with nonphysical consciousness. Both researchers have also shown, under stringent triple blind protocols, that skilled mediums provide accurate and specific information about deceased and living people without any prior knowledge of the deceased or their family. (Many of their technical papers are freely available online.) Beischel is now directing her work towards studying the therapeutic benefits of mediumship while Schwartz continues to research bigger questions, such as the role that dead play in our lives and how great minds might continue to contribute to humanity, even after death.

I must say here that given the current state of research and thinking on the topic of human consciousness, and recent advances in research, it is no longer acceptable to sit back and label oneself a skeptic whenever a topic such as survival of consciousness, telepathy, spiritual experiences or mediumship comes up, as if anyone who doesn't accept that the world only works in the ways dictated by either materialist or religious dogma is delusional or naive. Considering the caliber of work by researchers, philosophers, physicists and other visionaries investigating consciousness, claiming to be a skeptic without having familiarized yourself with at least some of the current research is like asserting superiority by virtue of one's own ignorance. Furthermore, doing so is not only ignorant and rude, it prevents open discussion and creates an environment of intolerance towards anyone who has had an extraordinary or nonmaterial experience.

The general intolerance towards open discussion and exploration of existential issues by those who declare themselves to be skeptics over the last few decades continues to have deleterious effects on people's health and well-being.[18] When extraordinary, spiritual, or sacred experiences do occur, our first reaction should be wonder and appreciation, not fear. We should not automatically fear the unknown, let alone for our sanity when extraordinary experiences occur. These experiences should light us up, recharge and inspire us. Instead, many people are forced to live in fear of an essential, fundamental part of themselves, their natural abilities, and of what will happen to them if they talk about their experiences. No one should have to hide extraordinary and sacred experiences for fear of being judged, ridiculed, persecuted or discriminated against by self-declared skeptics, and people who think they know better.

Some people's seemingly outlandish beliefs and explanations for extraordinary phenomena are such a confusing distraction that it's easy to dismiss them out of hand and entirely overlook the value and validity of their knowledge and skills. I think ability and very real experiences are all too often dismissed because of packaging, linguistics, and imagined implications: people might believe ex-military personnel who say they used remote viewing to gather intelligence or scientists who say that they have observed and measured precognition in multiple labs around the world,[19] but will completely dismiss shamans who talk to plant spirits or psychics who say that angels tell them about the future even though they are all dealing with essentially the same ability.

I will humbly suggest here that a concise, baggage free vocabulary makes conversations about consciousness and telepathy more productive, and would go a long way to making these abilities more accessible and useful, as well as deepening our collective wisdom. However, words are not the important thing. It's what words point to that is important. Once you grasp the meaning words point to, forget the words, they will hold you back and warp your true understanding of what they once pointed to. Hold onto the words that describe and point to consciousness and the etheric world and you will be left with empty concepts to argue over, and no true understanding whatsoever.

Once you have spent a little time in your connected mind (and you all have) or had a sacred experience, many truths and understandings become self-evident, and the words you use to describe experiences in the connected mind won't really matter. Words and explicit definitions will become unimportant. You might hear what all the flaky people were actually saying for the first time, and realize they might not be delusional after all. You might even find your own conversations taking on a poetic expressiveness with like-minded people, where words are intentionally used in the wrong way, out of context, or metaphorically to point at greater understandings that are clear to everyone listening in a state of connection.

You may also find yourself using vague and metaphorical words like *energy* a lot, as in: "Her energy is really grounded, but she's still got that sparkly kid-like energy. She really changed the energy of the room when she showed up, I got so energized, I really have a lot of energy to burn off now." We have to admit, it's a problem. Our modern vocabulary is almost entirely structured around the material world, as we have ignored our telepathic experience of the world for centuries. Our culture very much lacks a concise vocabulary when it comes to describing consciousness and our experiences with consciousness, so metaphor and poetic license become necessary to describe basic truths about the essence of things. Poetic license also keeps us free from the trap that words can become; by constantly using different words to point to greater meanings, we run less danger of warping our true understanding of things with unwanted baggage.

Using poetic license, however, we run the risk of sounding ungrounded, unable to commit to, relate to or concisely speak about anything substantial. We can become unbalanced, unable to effectively function or get anything done in the material world we have to live in. This is common with many people who can't balance their spiritual experience of the world with the material world, and have difficulty establishing boundaries, competently holding down a job, managing money, or maintaining stable relationships. This imbalance is a common symptom of spiritual bypass, a condition that many people fall into when they first open up to connection through spirituality. They only focus on greater meanings and their feelings are from the heart up, and in so doing, they become completely ungrounded. Everything becomes a sign and the literal meaning of events and even straightforward conversation is lost. The connected mind and all things etheric can be incredibly useful and life enhancing, when grounded and integrated into real life. Focusing solely on the spiritual and etheric, however, can be detrimental, although probably less harmful than focusing only on the material.

Similarly, only looking to science for vocabulary and understanding the world can also be detrimental. Science is one perspective through which we can understand ourselves and the world; an immensely valuable method of acquiring, communicating and integrating knowledge. The perspective science gives us on the world is, however, very impersonal: an intellectual perspective that can only provide us with limited conceptual understandings of the world. If we only look to science for understanding as to the nature of consciousness, we will never get beyond our thinking, plotting, manipulating survivor minds. We will never go from believing to knowing, and never really understand the nature of our own minds, or the amazing and wonderful abilities we all have (but mostly insist we don't).

To get beyond conceptual understandings, we need to completely let go of objective perspectives, let ourselves experience rather than theorize, and know rather than believe. We need to get out of our own heads for awhile, out of our thinking minds and into our connected minds. There are mountains and oceans in the backyard of our own minds, if we dare to let ourselves notice, and personal proof that our minds are not isolated in our brains is readily available and attainable for anyone who is willing to open their mind and check it out.

Reading the rest of this guide, and maybe for a few moments each day from now on, I ask that you try to let go of what you know about the material world, and material definitions. I ask that you concern yourself with what words point to rather than explicit definitions or conceptual ideas. I ask that you stop insisting that anyone, yourself included, who sees, experiences, speaks of or believes in unseen forces, influences or beings is delusional or naive. I ask that you let yourself get a little messy in the playground of your connected mind, that you notice and play with your own strange and random thoughts, and consider how they may be connected to the wider world.

I ask that you play with the idea that part of your mind, your connected mind, is not in your brain, and never was, so it survives the demise of the physical body, and it is capable of doing extraordinary things. This idea has proven to be freeing, comforting and powerful. It's a simple idea but one that eases existential fear by helping people understand themselves and their place in the universe. By resisting the idea that part of our minds exists, whether or not we have a physical body, and that our minds are connected to one another and the wider world, we cut ourselves off from understanding an essential part of ourselves, the world and our natural abilities. The instant we become aware of this part of ourselves, what I call the connected mind, our world changes: life takes on a new depth and meaning, new possibilities and connections emerge, and we can reconnect with our sense of awe and appreciation for the wonder of life. We naturally begin to use the latent but very innate abilities of the connected mind in our own unique ways and begin to live life on another level altogether.

Once you wrap your head around the idea that part of your mind, your connected mind, is not only not in your brain, it is not even in the physical world – so it is not bound by the laws of physics that apply to physical matter or ordinary cause and effect – many extraordinary abilities like telepathy, clairvoyance and mediumship begin to make sense. When we begin to understand the mechanics of the connected mind, and can explain its functioning in clear straightforward terms, paranormal phenomena become understandable, benign, normal, interesting and even useful. Once this happens, developing and using your own extraordinary abilities becomes a real possibility. When we begin to truly understand where our connected mind is, how to focus with it and what we perceive with it, life becomes a magical place, but the magic is very real. Although learning, or more accurately remembering, how to use your connected mind is a personal journey, requiring practice and plenty of trial and error, it is a journey made easier when you know you are not alone, that you are not crazy, and have some context to help you understand your experiences.

Part II – The Connected Mind

The Survivor Mind – A Toolbox for Physical Reality

Until you make the unconscious conscious, it will direct your life and you will call it fate.
~ CG Jung

To get telepathic information or communicate with other beings, I still the thoughts of my survivor mind and wonder about whatever I want to know about. The ability is natural and innate, and the process is really and truly that simple for everyone. The process is about becoming receptive, noticing that your brain is an antenna or receiver as well as a logic engine. Everyone slips into receptive states from time to time, usually by accident, and everyone can learn to do this at will by bringing awareness to the process and consciously practicing. I often compare the sensation to the moment that the lights go down in a theatre, everyone goes quiet and you patiently wait with curious anticipation for the movie to start. At the theatre, you don't go get the movie, the movie comes to you. In that place, you are receptive.

If your mind is quiet and receptive, whenever you wonder with gentle curiosity, the images, sensations or understandings that pop into your awareness will be real information about whatever you are wondering about, not just your own thoughts or imagination. The part of my mind that I quiet to become receptive, the survivor mind, is easier to see once I have stepped outside of it and can look back to see it for what it is. Once my mind is quiet and receptive, this usually noisy part of other people's minds also becomes easy to see. Helping people understand this noisy part of themselves and see how it can suck the joy out of life by creating repeating patterns of stress and drama is a part of the connected mind work I do. Understanding your survivor mind isn't the important part though, understanding that you are *not* your survivor mind, and recognizing when you are, and are not, in your survivor mind is the important part. To understand the connected mind, and how to get into your connected mind, we have to begin with the biggest barrier – the survivor mind.

Most of us live pretty full time in our survivor minds, but the survivor mind is only a toolbox for living in the mundane physical world. It includes functions that popular psychology refers to as left brain. It brings order to your world by categorizing and judging the massive flow of information being taken in by your physical senses. It sequentially runs thought scenarios, searching past experiences and projecting those experiences into the future and onto others to make decisions, keep you safe, and avoid repeating any pains from the past. Its one and only aim is to improve your chances of survival by avoiding anything it deems negative or potentially harmful, and attempting to control resources that might improve your chances of survival, including other people.

The survivor mind learns from experience, coming to conclusions about the world and its place in it. You might call these conclusions judgements, rules, beliefs or even subconscious beliefs, depending on the degree to which a survivor mind generalizes, clings to, or emotionally charges them. Some rules like "don't touch hot things" work well, while other rules like "people can't be trusted" unconsciously play out in our lives in unwanted ways, creating repeating loops of negative experiences that reinforce the validity of the rule to the survivor mind.

Other survivor mind rules like "I'm responsible for keeping everyone safe", "I'm not good enough", or "People can't handle the real me" are typically developed in response to some kind of trauma (big or small). Living according to these types of survivor mind conclusions can be incredibly destructive. Survival strategies learned early in life that revolved around being weak, sick, broken, conforming, silent or invisible, so as not to pose a threat, or to gain attention, acceptance and protection from survivor mind oriented family and community members, can be particularly destructive. Such beliefs tend to cyclically play out in unpleasant ways, long after we have left the environments that created them, distracting us from the natural ease and flow of life by creating needless, stressful, energy-draining drama. Living with a noisy survivor mind requires huge amounts of attention and focus, leaving little time or energy for productive co-creation, playing in the moment, and the simple joys of living, being and exploring the world.

You could call this part of the mind the ego, persona, or thinking mind. I call it the survivor mind because when it's not consciously directed towards other purposes, its one and only function is to maximize its chances of survival on this planet. As a result of the society we have created, your survivor mind sees you as a vulnerable, finite, separate being competing for power over limited resources. It sees the world and everything in it, including other beings and people, as resources for survival, or threats to its safety, no matter how safe and abundant life actually is. It is never satisfied or fulfilled. It only knows how to judge, assess and project thought scenarios to seek more power, influence, safety and control. It comes at life from a place of lack, scarcity, and conditionality.

Even some of what we consider our most benign and altruistic thoughts can sometimes be traced back to the impetus of competing for survival. Money, our social status and reputation, our friends, our intimate relationships, our homes, our looks, who we know, where we go, what we know, and even our loved ones, can become things to be possessed and used by our survivor mind for a sense of power and control. The more lost in the survivor mind people are the more likely they are to objectify people, animals or the environment and manipulate, lie, cheat, steal or worse to keep themselves safe from mostly or entirely imagined threats, however remote.

It's not that the survivor mind is an inherently bad thing; it can be a wonderful toolkit of know-how, and useful rules, provided it doesn't take over and run your entire life. It's a necessary and useful part of ourselves. We need it for tasks like crossing the street and grocery shopping. Its survival software is essential for functioning in the physical world, but it can trip into overdrive, and can't be shut off, especially in competitive or stressful environments, social isolation and following traumatic events. All too often, we forget to turn it off, and it takes over our lives before we realize what has happened.

Understanding that the survivor mind's only function is survival can help you to step back from your survivor mind and see it for what it is, rather than mistaking it for who you are. Once you understand the inner workings of the survivor mind, you shine a light onto previously unconscious ways of being, not only creating self-awareness and opening access to other more powerful parts of your mind, but also creating the freedom to consciously choose the life you want rather than getting the life you're driven to.

The survivor mind is such an exceptional toolbox, and its solutions to survival so ingenious, it is easy to mistake our survivor minds for a wise and knowing part of ourselves. You can think of the survivor mind as a state of being where the most primitive part of the mind, what science understands as the reptilian brain, insidiously takes control and directs, towards its own ends, the intelligence of the higher brain. Your abstract thinking, critical reasoning, creative intelligence and intuitive powers all become focused onto a singular, illusionary purpose: getting your needs met to ensure survival. To make matters worse, when the survivor mind takes over, it hijacks the power of the connected mind to telepathically orchestrate and draw us toward desired life experiences. Rather than bringing intended and desired experiences into our lives, the hijacked connected mind unconsciously directs us towards survival-based dramas and orchestrates painful experiences that reinforce our survivor mind beliefs.

With the stresses of modern life, and a pervasive news media that does its best to convince us that potential threats to our survival are everywhere, and evolving, with new threats appearing daily, the survivor mind trap is insidiously easy to fall into. The process is slow, quiet and convincing, so we rarely realize that we've become trapped within our own survivor minds. The condition has become so pervasive, that it is the new normal.

When we become enamored with the projections and dramas of the survivor mind, or lose the desire and ability to quiet it, we can no longer see it for what it is, and over time we begin to mistake it for who we are. We lose our sense of belonging, can no longer see beyond our own projections and the world as it actually is. We lose ourselves in conditional love and dramas of our own making, seeing only our desires and fears, no matter how abundant or how safe our lives are, or how remote the dangers are. The moment that the thought scenarios of our survivor minds become more real to us than the real world is the moment we become unconscious in our lives.

The irony of the survivor mind is that it can become the greatest threat to its own survival on both an individual and collective level. By taking control and cutting off access to the connected mind, the survivor mind destroys our ability to see ourselves in others, our capacity for empathy, cooperation, true ingenuity, unconditional love and symbiotic co-creativity. The survivor mind's understanding of the world is very limited, based only on fear, base desires, its past experiences (in life or through the media), and its logical extrapolations. The survivor mind becomes dangerous when it mistakes its tiny ideas of the world for the real world and believes that it needs to control, can control, or is in control of the external world. It is only in connection with others and the wider world that long-term survival of any one person or group is possible, but the survivor mind isn't capable of connection. Separateness and selfishness are hardwired into the survivor mind. It can only see the world from the perspective of resources and threats to a biological entity requiring nourishment, protection from the elements, safety from attack and the ability to reproduce.

Most of us don't recognize the survivor mind in ourselves, or others, because we have refined our survivor minds by educating them. We have disguised our basic survival drives with civilized vocabulary and complex sets of concepts such as law, economics, philosophy and etiquette. The survivor mind is not the same mind that indigenous peoples and hunter-gatherer cultures use to survive in nature. Survival in nature requires intuition through connection with others and with nature. I perceive many modern indigenous peoples and present day hunter-gatherers as still living mostly in their connected minds, in connection with nature and one another. They live quietly and in ways that we might perceive as simple, or backward, but many of us can't stop talking, thinking or judging for long enough to notice the depth of their existence.

I perceive the survivor mind as having developed and evolved along with agrarian cultures where competition arose between humans for the resources they perceived as limited; resources that could be stored, hoarded and meted out by those in control. The survivor mind is therefore driven by concepts of ownership, limited supply and justice: concepts that would be nonsensical to pre-agrarian societies where survival depended on the communal ability to live in connection and harmony with one another and the infinite abundance of nature.

The survivor mind takes control by not shutting off, or by insisting that the connected mind either does not exist or is something to be feared. Fortunately, the survivor mind can be convinced to relinquish control, relax and shut down for a while, especially if it begins to trust that the connected mind not only exists, but is also a friendly and beneficent part of the self that can be relied on to create safety and abundance. Luckily, the connected mind's ability to orchestrate serendipitous occurrences, synergistic relationships, know the future, synchronistically inspire and guide one's actions away from danger and towards desired outcomes makes *it* the ultimate survival tool. Escaping the survivor mind is not only about avoiding stress, conflict and ecological armageddon though. Living solely in your survivor mind is sort of like choosing to drive a slow, smelly, gas-guzzler with uncomfortable seats, and an AM radio when you've got a luxury electric super car in the garage.

The survivor mind operates sequentially, linearly and logically. Its sequential operation makes it very slow in comparison to the connected mind; slow enough that we can easily watch the survivor mind working. When the survivor mind is all that we focus on, it is easily and often mistaken for who we are. Realizing that you are not your survivor mind because you are observing it functioning, and therefore the observer and not what is being observed, is the first step to understanding and escaping the survivor mind. In contrast to the slow survivor mind, the connected mind functions so quickly and intuitively that most people don't notice it functioning at all. It is who we are, and what we perceive the world with, so observing the connected mind is sort of like trying to observe your own eyeballs.

Once we know where and how to pay careful and consistent attention though, we can bring conscious awareness to our connected minds. With careful and directed attention, we can learn how to use our connected minds to get information about, learn about and understand anything we want, from the inside out, including our own survivor minds. Focusing only on the day to day functioning of our survivor minds, and their constant streams of thought scenarios, most of us are only aware of our survivor minds' surface functioning. We aren't consciously aware of the lifetime of judgements, beliefs and fears lurking below the surface of the iceberg of our survivor mind, waiting for ships to wreck.

The sum total of our life learnings, experiences and traumas, everything our parents warned us about, we've seen in the movies or have been taught in church or school, is buried in and hoarded by our survivor minds. Our survivor minds like nothing more than to pull out a learning from the past to protect us, or make us more powerful, whether or not the situation warrants it or doing so makes sense. Many of our survivor minds' learnings are highly useful for functioning on the planet, in the right context. Unfortunately, the survivor mind often has difficulty letting go of what it thinks it knows, and often applies rules and beliefs in contexts and situations far outside of where they were originally learned, or long after they have proved ineffectual, with disastrous results.

When you can no longer quiet your survivor mind, life becomes stress. Although its effects are very real, stress itself is an illusion, created by and existing solely within the survivor mind. Stress is a result of our perception of how things should be, and resistance to how things are. It is the survivor mind directing attention, energy and resources to address perceived threats to its power and position, pulling you away from the present moment and from your connected mind, which is far more capable of creating safety, abundance, peace and joy in your life. The greater the perceived threat or need, the more the survivor mind will demand your attention, suck your energy and pull you into thought scenarios about the past and future.

Everybody at one time or another has had a problem or experience they can't stop thinking about, or replaying in their head, until the problem is solved, or the experience is integrated. In the most extreme cases, this state of persistently intrusive thought is labeled posttraumatic stress disorder, in milder cases most people call it worry. The more the survivor mind's thought scenarios are at odds with what is, or what has been, the greater the perceived threat and resultant demand for energy and attention. Stress, then, can simply be seen as a direct measure of the degree to which our survivor minds are turned on, and the degree to which they are at odds with how things are.

The survivor mind is the ultimate addict. Left unchecked, it will endlessly identify more and more things to be acquired, owned or controlled, and more threats to worry about. When a possession, ability, strategy, role or substance has made a survivor mind feel powerful and safe, a stressed survivor mind will return to it again and again. When we don't turn our survivor minds off, or actively choose a better focus, they endlessly drive us to repeatedly use substances, strategies, and roles that worked once upon a time, even if they no longer work or have become detrimental to our lives and health.

Stress diverts our energy toward solving perceived threats and problems, away from the present moment, creating enjoyable life experiences and healing the body. In the short-term, this energy drain can feel energizing and empowering to our survivor minds. Physiologically, the body's fight or flight mechanisms are turned on, muscles are primed for action and our senses are heightened to detect and anticipate threats. Repair and maintenance of the body slows or stops to make energy available for fight or flight. We lose the ability to sense the subtler needs of our body, mind and spirit, and the needs and wants of others. We ignore or become completely unaware of the body's requests for nutrition, rest or movement and the mind's requests for stimulation, novelty and connection. We cut off our connection to the greater whole and the natural flow of information that allows us to function with wisdom in synergy and symbiosis with other beings and the planet.

Numbing substances such as alcohol, nicotine, sugar, refined carbohydrates and other painkillers provide a temporary reprieve from a demanding survivor mind, but this numbing further reduces our ability to sense our subtler needs and connect with others. If energy is chronically diverted away from healing the body, the joy of play and fulfilling connection, ageing accelerates, the body becomes prone to infection and disease, or the immune system turns on itself. The constant demand of a survivor mind that never shuts off depletes the body and mind until one or the other breaks.

Breakdowns occur when all of your coping strategies have stopped working or all of your energy is drained. The sense of overwhelm from the demands of a convincing survivor mind and the constant energy drain that comes with it can often work to wear down your resilience to life. Some people get sick, anything from a cold to cancer, while other people go into depression or have a nervous breakdown. Many people think of breakdowns as a break from sanity when really the opposite is often true. Breakdowns offer tremendous opportunities to escape the grip of the survivor mind and return to consciousness, sanity and well-being. I think of a nervous breakdown as an etch-a-sketch moment in life; a rare chance to consciously rewrite broken beliefs, establish new boundaries and reestablish what you want, who you actually are and your place in the world.

Breakdowns don't have to be publicly messy events that disrupt your entire life and draw concern from friends, family and coworkers though. You don't need to wait for the big one to address what you know are your issues. You can take yourself on with intention and awareness, clean up your past and bring closure to old events in manageable, fulfilling chunks with a conscious friend, coach, therapist, sponsor, shaman or on retreat where breakdowns are called breakthroughs. When there aren't so many broken parts of your life jumping up and demanding your attention all the time, and those unresolved events from your past don't become the seeds of why you should run from the relationship you are currently in for example, your survivor mind isn't nearly as convincing. On the other side of such introspective work, you return to life renewed, rejuvenated, calmer, wiser and with better boundaries.

If we don't stay conscious of its functioning, and we lose ourselves in its dramas, the survivor mind becomes who we are. We end up an unconscious participant in the world, sleepwalking through life as fearful, coveting, manipulating and mistrusting egos that judge, compare, separate and blame. Breaking down the survivor mind from this sort of vigilant, fearful state requires courage and determination. It can feel utterly terrifying because you really and truly feel like you are dying, especially if you are not consciously aware that your survivor mind and its thoughts are not you. During this process, a part of you is dying; the collection of rules and ideas that makes up your survivor mind and your persona, your judgements and beliefs about yourself and the world, are being torn apart piece by piece. Don't worry though, your survivor mind will rise again… and again, and again.

If you are willing to break down the outdated rules and beliefs that make up your survivor mind, you have the opportunity to examine them piece by piece, and see your projections for what they are and how they came to be. Seeing your survivor mind from outside of itself, you start to see how it isn't you, and you can find new meaning in the story of your life. This is your opportunity to understand yourself on a deep level, and recreate yourself as you wish. You can consciously choose which pieces of your survivor mind are to be kept, amended, or abandoned altogether, and consciously choose new rules, beliefs and values.

The resurrection and transformation of the survivor mind may seem like the important part of a breakdown; after all, this is a central story in many religious teachings and the focus of most mental health professionals. You can make your survivor mind a better and better survivor mind, but it is still your survivor mind. Focusing solely on building a better survivor mind can further strengthen its grip on your life. Purely intellectual efforts at self-improvement can further entrench you in your survivor mind, because they reinforce the survivor mind's illusion that it knows everything and is in control. The part of a survivor mind breakdown that is most uncomfortable, that many people direct their energies towards trying to avoid altogether, and is often looked upon as a sign of weakness or illness, is the most important, valuable and sacred part: the part where you feel like you are dying and have nothing left to cling to. The moment when everything you once thought was you is broken, torn apart, or has dissolved is one of the most powerful moments in life, and ironically, one of the best opportunities to find true serenity.

When you learn how to die, you learn how to live. If you can get past the existential terror of the death of the ego, of your survivor mind having nothing left to cling to, even for a moment, the first thing that you'll notice is that you still exist! The second thing you will notice, if you're open to it, is profound peace and relief. The moment you escape your survivor mind is the moment I encourage people to strive for, in whatever form it takes. Breaking down the survivor mind is not the only way to quiet it though, and certainly not the most pleasant way into the connected mind. There are many, many ways into the connected mind because it is who we are, and where we find ourselves when we are not focusing on physical reality and our survivor minds. Once we get familiar with the sensation of being in our connected minds, we can consciously choose to be in either part of ourselves at will. Getting to the point where we can consciously and comfortably slip between survivor mind and connected mind is largely a matter of practice.

The Connected Mind

The creative act is a letting down of the net of human imagination into the ocean of chaos on which we are suspended, and the attempt to bring out of it ideas. It is the night sea journey, the lone fisherman on a tropical sea with his nets, and you let these nets down – sometimes, something tears through them that leaves them in shreds and you just row for shore, and put your head under your bed and pray. At other times what slips through are the minutiae, the minnows of this ichthyological metaphor of idea chasing. But, sometimes, you can actually bring home something that is food, food for the human community that we can sustain ourselves on and go forward.

~ Terence McKenna

When we manage to quiet our survivor minds and shift our focus away from the physical world we see with our eyes, away from our constructed identities and the perspective of the brain between our ears, we find ourselves where we always were, in our connected mind. In comparison to the constant noise and drama of the survivor mind, the profound peace of the connected mind can seem like an empty void at first, but the connected mind is far from empty. What we find there is far more subtle than the physical reality we are used to. It is ethereal and ephemeral, and easily drowned out by the thoughts, projections and imaginings of our survivor minds. It may seem like there's nothing there, yet, once we learn to focus, what we find there can be so rich and intimate that it can be overwhelming and far more intense and powerful than physical world experiences.

If you can stay out of the judgements, expectations and thought scenarios of your survivor mind, and your imagination, you will notice that in your connected mind, your awareness is filled with sensory experiences and knowings that can look and feel like a daydream whenever you gently wonder, or focus on something. The information you get is sensory: sight, sound, taste, smell or touch and is often accompanied by feelings and knowings. You may feel and locate the sensations in your body, however, there is no physical stimulus. Paying attention to your body, especially subtle feelings and sensations in your gut and heart, is a powerful and common way into the connected mind. I use the terms *inner* or *subtle sensory* to distinguish nonphysical sensory information from information about the physical world obtained through our physical senses.

The connected mind is a subtle sensory environment: there are no words there. Instead of words, sensory information is often accompanied by a knowing or awareness, what I call *clairiscience* (pronounced klair-ish-*uh*-ns, as in omniscience; not to be confused with *clairsentience* – feeling something psychically, either emotionally or kinesthetically). Clairiscience is a sort of instantaneous understanding of what you are focusing on, or aspects of it. You can think of clairiscience as being two steps down from omniscience which suggests spontaneous knowledge of everything simultaneously.

Through clairiscience, you know things spontaneously through your connected mind alone, but you only know about what you are focusing on within the parameters of your curiosity or intention. What we find in the connected mind does not necessarily contain perfect or complete information about any given subject. People often confuse telepathy and psychic abilities with the concept of omniscience; not understanding how telepathy and the connected mind works, they use faulty logic to dismiss such abilities, concluding that if someone doesn't know everything, or hasn't won the lottery for example, then they aren't psychic.

Clairiscience occurs so quickly and effortlessly, most of us don't notice how often we naturally and effortlessly use telepathy to grasp clairiscient understandings during everyday conversations and interactions. Telepathic and energetic conversations always accompany verbal conversations and physical interactions, and we often grasp meaning before or while words are being spoken, without processing or even paying attention to their direct meaning. Telepathic and energetic exchanges are actually going on all the time, whether we are conscious of them or not. When such exchanges do slip into our awareness, we often mistake them for our own thoughts. Once you are aware of clairiscience, and your ever-present telepathic connection to the world, you can bring consciousness to this innate ability, and over time learn to use it with more and more skill, and discern clairiscience from your survivor mind's judgements. You can also learn to translate the implicit understanding of clairiscience into explicit words and concepts, making what you find in the connected mind more useful to yourself and others in the physical world.

At first, it can be difficult to tell the difference between your imagination and your connected mind. Your imagination feels very similar to the connected mind because it's a sensory environment, just like your connected mind. The difference is that your imagination originates with you. It is more connected to your survivor mind's thought scenarios and projections than it is to anything outside of you. The thought scenarios and imaginings of the survivor mind are linear extrapolations of the survivor mind's past experiences, and its constructed understanding of the world; essentially 'what if' scenarios. In the connected mind, you find real, authentic, actual information, from outside of your own mind, about whatever you wonder about, without exception. Whenever you wonder about something related to a real person, place, thing or subject, you will get real and relevant information in response to your curiosity. The ability to discern your imagination from your connected mind, to separate your own thought projections from what you see in your connected mind, is the key to making telepathic information reliable, useful and valuable.

Gentle curiosity, desirelessness and calm focus are the keys to staying in your connected mind and out of your own imagination. Try too hard in the connected mind and your effort becomes an obstacle to seeing clearly. Trying is a survivor mind behavior based in fear: fear of needs not being met, fear of failing, of being wrong, or what people might say *or* think. *Try* in your connected mind, and your imagination will fill in all the scenarios that you desire or fear. There is no trying in the connected mind. It is as it is. There is no manipulating to get what you want, no failure, no danger and there are no needs to be met.

Whenever you focus with intention, if you can't completely let go of your fear of being wrong, or desire to get a certain answer, your imagination will fill your awareness with thought scenarios reflecting your fears and desires, clouding your perception of the connected mind. Consequently, *try* to get information in the connected mind and the information you get will only reflect your own desires and fears, though you might not realize it, as the information will still appear very real. Real information can only be seen from a receptive, desireless and non-attached state when your survivor mind is silent and your connected mind is cleanly and gently experiencing whatever your pure intent and curiosity has brought you to. Let answers come to you, staying as calm, objective and as uninvested in the outcome as possible.

If you've ever watched a scary movie, or an awkward comedy that made you uncomfortable enough to resist the plot direction and think: "no, don't go in there" or "don't do that" – as if you can psychically will the characters to make good choices from the couch in a movie that has already been made – you understand the sensations of resistance and of observing with desire or fear. Observation in the connected mind is very much like watching a movie, except that your resistance, desires or fears actually change what you observe and perceive in the connected mind.

If you can simply sit back and watch what shows up in your mind, you'll experience and perceive its true nature in its fullness with detail. You'll also realize the futility of trying, resisting, wishing and fearing. This doesn't mean that you should watch every movie you see, or everything that pops into your mind. Clear, beneficent intentions along with firm and vigilant boundaries are essential when venturing into the connected mind or any altered states of consciousness. Every experience and possibility can be experienced in its fullness in the connected mind at the speed of thought. You can't unexperience, just as you can't unsee, and some experiences are hard to shake off and leave behind. I highly suggest filling your mind with experiences and information that light you up, not traumas and injustices that drag you down.

The reason you get actual information about whatever you wonder about or focus on in your connected mind is that your focus actually connects you with whatever you're wondering about, the real thing, through what I refer to as that thing's *subtle reality*. In the connected mind, there is less separation between you and everything else than there is in the physical world. So much less separation that, away from your imagination and your survivor mind, simply by focusing on, or wondering about something, your consciousness will merge with whatever you focus on. The more comfortable with this process you are, the longer and more intently you focus, the broader and deeper the merger will be.

This merging, union or yoking, as it is referred to in yoga philosophy, can be highly enjoyable, especially if you focus on themes, things or people that you find enjoyable or pleasurable. If you focus on something unpleasant though, depending on your proficiency, you will experience the fullness of its unpleasantness. What you focus on in the connected mind, you experience intimately and viscerally, from the inside out. Away from the survivor mind, with intent focus, what you experience in the connected mind can be just as vibrant, and far more intense or profound than ordinary physical experience. If a picture is worth a thousand words, perceiving with your connected mind and understanding something by merging your consciousness with it so you understand it from the inside out is worth a million. There simply aren't words to really explain the experience to anyone who has not ventured far enough outside of their own survivor mind to relate.

Regardless of what you focus on in the connected mind, whether it is unpleasant or profoundly beautiful, the experience of merging your consciousness can feel like a threat to the survivor mind, and the experience can be overwhelming at first. Most people never leave the confines of their survivor mind because it can feel strange or scary to do so, and merging your consciousness with something else can feel like you are leaving yourself behind with no way back, being consumed, or like your mind is being stretched to breaking. It's the same feeling that occurs during a nervous breakdown when the survivor mind is stripped away: you feel like you are dying. In a way you are dying; you are temporarily becoming something else, losing yourself in the consciousness of another thing or being, or whatever it is you are focusing on.

Comfort with this process of merging consciousness is central to the ability to obtain reliable information about whatever you want to know about, at will, with your connected mind. This is why the theme of death and becoming comfortable with your death is often central to shamanic traditions, and initiation as a shaman often requires that you experience your own death. Comfort with the process of dying and being without a body is also the reason that many people who have near death experiences become psychic; they have spent enough time away from their body and their survivor mind while clinically dead that they have become comfortable in their connected mind – like a bike they've never forgotten how to ride. The documented effects of people's near death experiences are telling and reassuring if you are considering exploring your connected mind: people consistently return to life after a near death experience with a greater sense of purpose and self-awareness, as well as a heightened sense of self-esteem, compassion for others, intuition and concern for the well-being of the planet.

This focus on death, dying and visceral unpleasantness may make it seem like the connected mind is an unpleasant and dangerous place. Getting out of your survivor mind to get to your connected mind can be a scary ordeal for many people, as the process can bring up many survivor mind issues: fears, anger, shame and sadness. From an outside survivor mind perspective, the process can look crazy, dangerous and terrifying. To proficiently access and use your connected mind in a wide variety of situations requires fearlessness, a strong sense of self, having faced your own issues and fears, and constant personal growth work. There is, however, nothing inherently unpleasant or dangerous at all about the connected mind itself. It's just the opposite. Living in our survivor minds, isolated in our own heads, lacking real connection and understanding of anything outside of ourselves is far more dangerous. Though living in isolation in our own minds can feel safe for a time, it inevitably becomes painful and unpleasant. The only trauma we find getting to the connected mind stems from our own fears, our mistaken belief that we are our survivor minds, and our survivor minds' vigilance against relinquishing control.

It is true that what you experience in your connected mind will change you forever, sometimes in ways that you might not anticipate or expect. What changes most as you venture into your connected mind though is your separateness, along with the pain, unease and angst of a random and meaningless existence that comes with feeling cut off, separate and alone. Living in separateness in your survivor mind does seem to make life easier.

You can act in ways that hurt and harm others, and yourself, seemingly without consequence, either because you are entirely unconscious of the effects of your actions, or because others' difficulties or pains do not seem to affect you. You can rationalize almost any behavior or decision, how you think things should be and how others should behave. In separation, to a survivor mind seeking power to control limited resources and its physical safety, the hardships, weaknesses and even the pain of others can be comforting and even pleasurable; assurance of power and survival. If you are truly in your connected mind, it is impossible to do anything that will harm another person or being, from an individual animal to an entire culture or ecosystem.[20] In your connected mind, you are much less separate from everything else. Harming what you focus on with your connected mind feels the same or worse than harming yourself.

Escaping your own survivor mind can be a difficult and sometimes painful process, particularly when we fear and resist this natural part of life. We don't, as a culture, mark, embrace, celebrate or work with the many inevitable transformations we each must go through in our lifetimes, when our survivor minds must be broken down to become something new. We seldom celebrate or help one another through life transitions, such as going from being a girl to being a woman, from being a boy to being a man, or from being a provider to being an elder.

To thrive through such transitions, to transform from who we were into who we want to be, and who we need to be, we have to step outside of our finite survivor minds, and allow our connected minds to inspire, guide and shape us into someone new. The logical survivor mind is for navigating the known and familiar, the connected mind is for transformation, and for navigating the new, novel and unknown. Rituals and traditions that offer community support and connection through dance, music and other means, thus permitting access into altered states and the connected mind, deserve great respect and consideration as tools for transition and transformation.

Venturing into the connected mind does not require breakdowns, community rituals or spiritual practice though. Getting comfortable in your connected mind can be done gradually and enjoyably through normal daily activities. Most people leave their survivor minds during leisure activities without consciously realizing what they are doing. Doing what you love is the best way to get out of your survivor mind, and has many positive side effects.

As you get more and more comfortable spending extended periods in your connected mind, away from your survivor mind, life becomes less stressful, and more enjoyable. Though enjoyable, pleasurable and fulfilling, doing what you love and escaping your survivor mind through leisure activities is far from frivolous. Ideas, insights and inspirations pop into your mind as if out of nowhere. The more you play in your connected mind, the more consciousnesses outside of yourself you connect with, the wiser and more conscious you become. The more you play in connection, allowing your consciousness to spread outside of your survivor mind, the less and less able you are to see yourself as separate from everybody and everything else on the planet. A profound sense of peace and belonging that everything is right in the world follows, as does the grace and luck that flow from living life in this connected way: when you are telepathically connected to many people and beings who intend cooperative co-creation, synchronicity and serendipity become a certainty rather than the whim of an unseen force or higher power.

Left to our own devices, playing and living life from our connected mind is something we all do naturally and spontaneously, especially as children. You know you are in your connected mind when you have lost yourself in what you are doing, whenever you lose your sense of time, or when you feel alive and inspired to play. Nature, music and movement are wonderful things to get lost in. Losing yourself in something much larger than yourself, like nature, or through shared experience is a lovely and comforting escape. Meditation and yoga are well-established and popular methods of escaping the survivor mind, and provide precise step by step methods for doing so. Classic methods of meditation are tricky for most people to deal with though. We are simply too stressed out, and our survivor minds too active for quiet pursuits like sitting cross-legged and following our breath while watching our thoughts and not attaching to them.

Adding an activity to meditation such as dance, yoga or music to keep your survivor mind busy often works well. Creative visualizations or chanting a mantra such as 'aaaaahhh' or 'aaauuuummm' work well to occupy and soothe the survivor mind, as does drumming, kirtan or playing an instrument. Exercise, sports, and creative pursuits such as writing, acting, painting, or photography all provide opportunities to lose yourself in the moment and connection, get out of your survivor mind so that, in the stillness that follows, you can see it, break down and remake it from outside in. If one is willing to be still, the survivor mind can also be lulled, allowing access to the connected mind. Lulling the survivor mind is something we do naturally and intuitively, especially for children through physical contact, gentle rocking, or bouncing. Simply watching the rhythm of waves or traffic can be just as effective for adults, and can be much like the swinging of a hypnotist's pocket watch, allowing you to alter your state and giving access to the connected mind.

Gateway to the Connected Mind Exercise

An excellent method to learn to discern your connected mind from your survivor mind is the tried and tested happy place or psychic room meditation. This creative visualization meditation is very commonly used to teach relaxation, introspection and psychic skills. To do the meditation, sit somewhere quiet. Cross-legged with good posture (your spine straight) is preferable, but lying down is fine too. Declare an intention, "to experience my connected mind for my highest good, and for the highest good of all" for example.

Breathe slowly and deeply with your diaphragm, pushing your belly out as you breathe in, then pulling it back towards your spine and up towards your rib cage when you breathe out, squeezing all of the air out of your lungs. Focus on your breathing for five or ten breaths. Follow your breath, letting it breathe you as much as you breathe it. Feel the sensation of simultaneously guiding and allowing your breath, of leading and following at the same time. Take this energy into your visualization.

As you relax, imagine a door. Imagining or intending as you inhale, focusing in the gap between breaths and then allowing and noticing as you exhale is an effective rhythm to slip into. Allow the door and everything else you imagine throughout the meditation to fill in with as much vivid detail and deeply sensory experience as you can. Use your imagination to fill in details but don't work hard. Let what shows up show up. Notice, without judgement or effort to change anything, unless anything unpleasant shows up, in which case firm boundaries and firm, deliberate effort to change your focus is appropriate. Use all five of your subtle senses. Notice any paint chips, subtle wood grains, or intricate metalwork on your door. Feel the texture of the door as you watch your finger slide along its surface towards the doorknob. Watch your hand close around the knob while you notice its temperature, shape and texture. Feel the resistance of the knob as you turn it, the weight of the door and the puff of air on your face as you open it.

On the other side of the door, imagine a happy, safe place coming into view. Your happy place can be a garden, a room, a beach, a park, a car, or whatever you like. Whatever pops into your head. As you walk through the door into your happy place, notice as many details as you can. Walk around and explore, taking in as many details and subtle nuances as you can, with as many senses as you can. Whatever you have to work hard to imagine, that takes time to fill in, or is vague and plain is likely coming from your imagination and survivor mind. Anything that pops into your mind instantaneously, with ease and vivid detail, is likely coming from your connected mind.

Visit your happy place often, daily if possible. Mornings are ideal, while your mind is fresh, and the house is quiet. Starting your day with meditation also anchors you in connection for the day, and is an opportunity to create your day by using your connected mind to guide and inspire your thoughts and decisions throughout your day towards desired goals and experiences. Initially, try to keep the environment in your happy place consistent over time. You want to be able to notice what changes and what shows up in the space you've created. Your happy place is essentially a framed canvas on which your connected mind can paint.

Entertain yourself in your happy place by inviting guests: famous people, people you admire or love, people you are curious about or made-up characters. If it delights you, fill your garden with animals, insects or pets (provided you don't feel any added stress from their presence). Have conversations with your guests. Interact with your animals and insects. At first you may feel silly, but keep at it until you lose yourself in your creations, and your creations take on a life of their own. When new people, animals, weather or things pop into your mind or show up in your happy place, or you find yourself in new places all of a sudden, notice everything you can. Notice what feels consistent day to day and what is new. Notice if sensations, objects, characters or pets in your happy place show up in response to a fear, desire or thought, or in response to a wondering or question, or out of nowhere.

As you spend time noticing the qualities of everything in your happy place, you can start to discern what you have to work to create with your imagination, and what your connected mind perceives effortlessly and instantly. The deeper and longer you lose yourself in your meditation, the more dreamlike the meditation becomes, the more it takes on a life of its own, the further into your connected mind you are. The sensory information that shows up with ease with vivid detail while you are lost in your meditation and takes on a life of its own is information from your connected mind, real information from outside of yourself that can become useful and even validatable if you can correlate it with the wondering, intention or questions that brought it to mind.

Explicitly write down questions or intentions each time you sit down to visit your happy place, and the information that shows up in response. Over time, you'll undoubtedly notice astounding correlations, find useful insights and information, and develop your own subtle sensory vocabulary. You may find that you no longer have to sit down and meditate, or go to your happy place to access your connected mind. You may notice your awareness filling with subtle sensory information throughout the day, whenever you slip into an altered state, or take a few centering breaths and gently wonder or daydream.

Whether you realize it or not, even if you have never meditated, you already spend time in your connected mind in a number of ways in your life. It is where many of us go to find solutions to difficult life problems, except that most of us come up with an excuse, or a cover story. Some people intuitively know to go for a run, clean, take a drive in the country, go somewhere sacred, or sleep on it, when they are wrestling with a tough situation, question or decision. When faced with a difficult problem, many of us naturally understand that we have to 'get out of our own heads' for a while to find a solution. By occupying our survivor minds for a while with a mundane task like driving, cleaning, or running, we can slip into connection to solve problems, find clarity or decide on a course of action.

The connected mind is who we are, so you know this place. You never completely leave your connected mind because it is who you are. It's just that most of us have become so entrenched in the constant crises created by our survivor minds, and enamored by the physical world, that we've learned to dismiss and ignore the connected mind experiences we're having all the time. Our connected minds are always there, always on, and even when we are deeply focused in our survivor minds, we are still cycling our awareness between our connected minds and our survivor minds. This cycling of awareness is something that we all do automatically, and so intuitively, we rarely notice it.

In normal waking states of consciousness, we spend more time in the survivor mind cycle of our awareness, focused in the physical world. The time we cycle into the connected mind is minimal and we don't usually notice the brief moments we cycle through our connected minds. With practice and discernment, it is possible to bring awareness to the tiny cycles of time you spend in your connected mind in waking life. This is essentially what psychics, mediums and other connected mind adepts are able to do: cycle into their connected mind with an intention or question and come back with information related to the question. Understanding what happens in the connected mind in this small space of time, how you find and perceive information, and how this information relates to the real world is the key to making the connected mind explicitly useful.

You can start to get familiar with your connected mind throughout your day by bringing more awareness to the organic ebb and flow of your survivor mind and connected mind, and noticing as your consciousness cycles between physical reality and subtle reality. In time, you will learn how to go with the flow and protract your experiences in the connected mind. Start by first noticing that, while your consciousness and awareness naturally cycles with its own rhythm, it also follows your focus, so you can protract your experiences through focus. Altering your state of consciousness can be thought of as expanding the cycle of time your focus is away from your survivor mind and physical senses, thus providing an expanded space of time to play in and familiarize yourself with the connected mind.

Getting into your connected mind is an evolving process, not a one-stop journey. Having your focus constantly return to your body, thoughts or imagination while meditating or altering your state in other ways is natural and not something to get frustrated over. Frustration pulls you out of the process. The key is to continually and gently pull your focus away from your survivor mind and physical senses. If you repeatedly focus away from the physical world, you will find yourself in your connected mind for longer and longer expanses of time and the universe of the connected mind will be your oyster.

During your time away, you can do many things, and what you do will depend on the intention or desire you entered your connected mind with. As I've said before and remind everyone of again, clear and positive purpose and intentions are the key to enjoying your experiences, staying safe, being productive and creating extraordinary results using altered states of consciousness and the connected mind. Regularly and explicitly declaring an intention like to *act for your highest good, for the highest good of everyone else involved, and for the larger whole,* along with a more specific intention or question, is essential when working in altered states and highly beneficial in any endeavor involving the connected mind.

Our connected minds are working all the time, whether we are aware of it or not, even when we sleep. The process of getting tired and sleeping can be understood from this framework as a peak in the natural and automatic cycling between the waking self in the physical world and the connected mind. Dreams can then be seen as the workings of your connected mind, and going to bed with a question or intention, then journaling first thing in the morning to remember and later analyze your dreams is a common way that many people already access the connected mind. What you see in the connected mind is very similar to what you seen in dreams, and making the information obtained through the connected mind useful is very similar to analyzing dreams. In both instances, you are translating subtle sensory information into meaningful symbols, words and concepts. The big difference is, in the wakeful connected mind, you can learn to be very precise whereas dreams mostly tend to be vague and often with general information overload.

When you learn to use your connected mind to obtain subtle sensory information in the moment, you do so by wondering about a specific topic or question. The information you bring back from your connected mind automatically has context: it relates to whatever you wondered about. You can spend time exploring, clarifying and validating the information you bring back as you go, and can ask multiple questions, returning to the connected mind again and again. With dreams, you are left to analyze a very big mishmash of half-remembered subtle sensory information with little if any context in which to understand it. If you want to ask another question, or get clarification, you have to wait until the next morning to get an answer.

Although sometimes the meanings of dreams are very clear, I'm not convinced that dream analysis is terribly reliable, prophetic or productive for the average person because of the lack of interactivity and context in which to understand the subtle sensory information dreams provide. I do think that the general vibe of your dreams offers valuable insight into the state of your life and mind, and that dream life is incredibly important. For me, my dream life has become a more and more enjoyable and fulfilling part of my life as I've become more conscious of my connected mind. Spending time and effort becoming more conscious in your dreams is a highly worthwhile pursuit. Thinking about, journaling and talking about your dreams is also an excellent place to practice recalling and translating subtle sensory information.

Most people understand how difficult it is to remember dreams. Sometimes we wake up with a vivid recollection of all kinds of details and plot lines from a dream, sometimes insights and understandings we know are profound, but moments later, we can't remember any of it, only a general vibe, or that there was something important in the dream. Recalling subtle sensory information from trips in the connected mind is similarly challenging. It's a skill that takes practice to learn. Telling someone about your dreams first thing in the morning is a good place to practice the process of translating connected mind information: you're translating sensory information into words, which can be far trickier than it may seem. Keeping a dream journal, as well as journaling before and after all of your intentional meditations and journeys into the connected mind, is an excellent way of making questions and wonderings, and the information you bring back in response to them, explicit and useful.

The practices of dream analysis, along with symbology, archetypal analysis, and critical analysis of art are also skills that transfer well to the connected mind, though not directly. In these practices, associative and analytical skills are applied to derive meaning from a dream symbol, image or story. For short intentional journeys into the connected mind from wakeful states, the meaning of the information you retrieve relates more directly to what you wondered about to get into the connected mind. Abstract analysis to figure out the symbolic meaning of a piece of information and how it relates to one's life is not usually required. Figuring out what a piece of information means isn't usually that challenging. Recognizing what you are perceiving or experiencing in the connected mind while you are there is the challenge, especially at first. Recognizing novel or unfamiliar thought forms and energies is always a challenge.

You certainly don't have to do any extra research, but having a broad knowledge of symbols, archetypes, stories and mythologies and associative-analytical skills can be helpful in *recognizing* subtle sensory information, in understanding what you are perceiving or experiencing with your connected mind. For example, a galaxy looks like a hurricane, looks like a nautilus shell, looks like a whirlpool: there is an essential nature to each of these objects that is very similar, if not identical. The subtle realities corresponding to each of these objects, the nonphysical part of these objects you can perceive with your connected mind, might *feel* or *look* very similar to your connected mind.

To differentiate the subtle reality of a galaxy from the subtle reality of a nautilus shell or whirlpool, you might have to engage multiple subtle-senses, and feel around from multiple perspectives with your connected mind to get multiple pieces of information that you can put together to understand what you are perceiving. Translating subtle sensory information and understanding what you are perceiving is sort of like the game show *The $10,000 Pyramid,* where contestants give one another hints and try to guess a word, hints like: popcorn, dark, seats, usher, from which you might guess "the movies".

From a cycling perspective, you can use your connected mind in two ways. One way is to expand the length of the cycle you are in your connected mind by altering your state of consciousness for extended periods of time. The second is to become consciously aware during the tiny expanses of time you naturally cycle through your connected mind in everyday life, and learn to perceive and discern subtle sensory information in the short time you are there. Becoming adept with your connected mind in life and in the moment largely depends on your ability to discern subtler and subtler sensory information in smaller and smaller frames of time; an ability that comes with time and practice in altered states.

Just spending time in altered states isn't really enough. Anyone can dream, meditate or trip out in other ways and have valuable, profound spiritual, psychic or psychedelic experiences. To become adept with your connected mind, to make your natural telepathic connection useful, valuable and real, you have to practice using your connected mind in those altered states by explicitly setting intentions, asking questions, obtaining information, writing it down or telling someone about it, and correlating that information with the physical world. In doing so, over time you will become more adept at navigating your connected mind, and you will be able to obtain more and more useful information from shorter and shorter durations in your connected mind. Over time, by constantly correlating your connected mind experiences with the real world, and continually noticing how subtle realities relate to physical reality, you will also develop a subtle sensory vocabulary, a lexicon through which you can automatically and intuitively translate subtle sensory experiences into meaningful physical world knowledge.

When I first started doing readings as a medium, I needed a half hour or more alone in darkness and silence to get information. At first, all of the information I received was visual, black and white images that looked like photo negatives on the back of my eyelids. I would lie down, cover my eyes and watch my eyelids like a movie screen, write down notes about the images I received, then share the information with whoever I felt like the information was for. Following that, I started meditating before sessions, getting some information, and working to stay in an altered state during my readings, so that I could get information in the moment for my sitters. I would often end up with a wicked headache, and would be completely drained after a single hour-long session. Over time, I needed to meditate and alter my state before readings less and less, and became more conscious of my connected mind in my daily waking life. The more conscious of my connected mind I was in daily life, the easier it became to correlate my inner experiences with my outer experiences – to understand how the subtle realities I was perceiving with my connected mind in any particular situation related to physical realities.

Working as a psychic medium, then as an animal telepath, afforded me many daily opportunities to correlate the subtle sensory experiences that arose in response to my wondering about something with people's lives and the physical world. Over time, by noticing how subtle sensory information correlates with real world issues in specific and consistent ways, I developed a better and better subtle sensory vocabulary, a sensory language through which I can understand, interpret and translate subtle sensory information. In the beginning, the process of going into subtle reality and following my curiosity was almost impossible to do when it came to getting information for myself, friends and loved ones.

Looking with your connected mind for information that is important to either your or a loved one's safety, career, reputation or monetary status tends to engage your survivor mind, which then warps the information you get in your connected mind because you can't help but be highly invested in the outcome. The higher the stakes, the more stressful the situation, or your life, the more desperate you or others are, the more your survivor mind kicks in and drowns out your connected mind. I have to say, I still struggle most getting specific and detailed information for myself, and the people closest to me, though not always. There are times when I can manage to be selfless and non-attached enough to allow myself to tread into the subtle realities of family if they feel they need it.

When it comes to yourself, family and friends, the more you can let go, and come at a question from a place of total non-attachment, objectivity, acceptance, allowance, abundance and playfulness, the easier it is to stay in connection, to let your body and mind flow to novel solutions, ideas and information. Noticing, recognizing and paying attention to information that shows up in the moment is key. The one and only time my eldest son ever asked me what the score of his upcoming football game would be, I couldn't tell him the score but I knew he would be injured. The very fact that he suddenly felt compelled to ask me to look at his game prompted both of us to pay attention. I knew that he would be injured, but couldn't bring myself to tell him not to play, only to pay attention and be careful. He finished a great game, but his knee blew up to twice the size right after, ending his season.

When my youngest son broke his clavicle snowboarding recently, I was out of the country, but he told me after that he knew he should have stayed home that day. A girl in his math class had randomly commented to him the day before how weird clavicles are, and they'd had a half hour conversation about how gross broken clavicles are. His stomach became suddenly upset before he left for the ski hill the next day. He pushed through and arrived to the news that his friend had just broken his clavicle. None of his friends were there, an oddity he noticed, and he didn't like the new changes to the board park jumps and rails. Nothing seemed right. He broke his clavicle after deciding he should leave after just one more run.

Synchronicities, oddities and our bodies speak to us very strongly when we are in connection and willing to pay attention. The subtle signs and sensations through which our connected minds speak to us are sometimes very hard to put together though, and only become clear in retrospect. The life lessons that teach us to pay attention to our connected minds can be tough; much like my childhood accident was for me. Learning to notice and trust your connected mind when the stakes aren't so high in situations where you can validate information after the fact can pay huge dividends in life. Every novel situation in life offers an opportunity to play with your connected mind, especially in regard to trivial matters that aren't about you. Noticing and playing in your connected mind regularly, and celebrating your successes, you will naturally come to trust and adeptly rely on your telepathic connection to the wider world in more important and personal situations through time. That doesn't mean that you can't lean into the connected mind to tackle big issues, pressing problems and important life decisions at any time though, with the help of a conscious and competent telepath, psychic, medium or shaman.

It's About Time – All Mushed Up

Learn how to see. Realize that everything connects to everything else.

~ Leonardo Da Vinci

Although I should be used to it by now, I am still amazed whenever someone contacts me to say: "Everything you told me came true!" I regularly receive such calls, many years after sessions, sometimes qualified with statements like: "I found your tape and listened to our session again. I'm sorry I gave you such a hard time, I didn't think there was any possible way I'd ever end up moving/breaking up/meeting someone/going back to school/changing careers. And there was a bunch of stuff I'd forgotten you said that all came true too." The lesson I learned early on in my work was to trust my ability and the information I get, even when the information seems completely crazy or a sitter insists in the moment that a piece of information doesn't belong to them or doesn't make sense.

I've had to say some really crazy things, for example: "Your dog is showing me the two of you climbing a flight of stairs above Thaifoon restaurant, but the stairs go my friend's apartment. My friend owns the restaurant, but his apartment is in a different part of town. It's a second story loft though, bedroom at the back, bright, living room overlooking the street." Sometimes things I have to say seem so crazy to me, or are so personal, that I almost can't bring myself to say the words.

In doing this work, part of my job is to advocate for the information I get by translating subtle sensory information as cleanly as possible while working with sitters to understand the information I'm getting, and why I'm getting it. I would be doing a great disservice if I just told my clients what they wanted to hear, or what I think would make sense. In the case of the dog showing me the Thai restaurant, his owner explained to me that she and her dog live in an apartment above a Vietnamese restaurant. Then she reminded me our call was long distance; she's wasn't local and didn't know the Thai restaurant I had mentioned, but she did confirm that her apartment stairs run up from a door in the front of a Vietnamese restaurant on the main street in her town, and that her living room overlooks the street, bedroom at the back, et cetera – a layout exactly like the layout of my friend's apartment that I'd described. Here, my mind had overlaid the closest resonant thing I knew onto what I was seeing telepathically, combining the dog's reality and places I knew into one picture. Incidentally, this story also illustrates one of the strange mechanics of the connected mind we will talk more about later: what you perceive with your connected mind is partly a projection of your own mind, ideas and thoughts.

When I look at possible futures for people, I do try and explain to them that I think of possible futures as visions that can be worked toward or away from, rather than absolute destinies – sort of like blueprints that our lives fill in around. I say this because I usually see multiple futures for clients that can change and shift as our sessions progress; different paths people can take, and the different futures that will result from different beliefs and choices. As people change their minds during my sessions, their possible futures also morph and change. Some clients don't have much going on at all in the way of possible futures when we first meet because they haven't made up their minds about anything, not even who they are and what they want in life. It often takes some time to work with such clients to get them back in touch with the part of themselves that longs for individual expression, from which co-creativity, joy, fulfilment and aliveness stem. Once these clients can get out of only living to please everyone else, doing what they 'should' do, and start thinking about what brings them joy and fulfilment, possible futures begin to emerge. Some of my sessions are as much about creating possible futures as they are about seeing them.

Some clients have one future that is very bright, clear and detailed in my mind. These are usually clients that are on a path or a mission, who have sometimes worked for years towards a particular goal, so aspects of their future are very clear. These images of a client's future can look predetermined as a result of their clear intentions and steady work. These are my favorite clients to work with. Their sessions are very productive because these clients are willing to lean into my skills and stretch my abilities to look far into the future to bring back helpful information and sort out the details of how various decisions, choices, or mindsets will affect their future plans, careers, relationships, health, etc.

I even have clients who borrow my skills for research and academic purposes, and the information I get sometimes gets so technical that I don't even know what we're talking about. Math was never my strong suit, but I've spent a fair amount of time talking to dead physicists, mathematicians and astronomers about some pretty esoteric and technical subjects. It's a very strange experience to say things, and not know what you're saying, but still have it make sense to the person you're talking to. The information I provide in these types of sessions makes sense to these clients and I know it pans out as I have worked with some of these clients over the span of several years. These sessions blur the lines between getting psychic information, looking at possible futures and mediumship, and the dead people who have shown up to help with topics like physics and astronomy have been very interesting to work with.

Most people I work with are faced with a few life choices, and subsequently have a few possible futures to sort through, pick from, and shape in more detail. For example, I might work with a client who is relocating and has their options narrowed down to a few houses or cities, and I can look at what their new life will look like in each new house or city. I know how my client will feel day to day in each new place, whether they are happy, healthy, how they spend their time. I usually see little scenes from their future life: older but fit and hiking with a new love interest, or depressed and alone at home flipping channels for example. I might see two or more versions of my client's life in one particular city though, and be prompted to say something like, "Los Angeles looks amazing! You're busy and fit and your food choices have shifted. Your work is thriving but you are going to have moments where you'll be suddenly exposed to some things you might not want to say yes to, like free drugs. Be careful. Temptation is high and the wheels can come off quickly if you don't stay consciously aware in these situations."

Possible futures look like lucid daydreams in my head, and so do people's past experiences, as well as their lives in the present, and because of that, I can't always tell where (or when) I'm looking. Usually I know if I'm in someone's past or future because I started a session with the intention to look at someone's future, or sort out an issue from the past. If we suddenly switch gears mid-session and decide to look at the future when we've been looking at the past, or if I follow an issue from the past to a connected future event, it can take me a second to get my bearings. Past and future feel the same and context is sometimes the only way I can figure out where I am, whether I'm in a client's past or in their future.

It's easy to understand that I'm looking at the past when I see someone as a child, or the future if someone is older. It's more challenging when I see scenarios that don't have any obvious temporal markers though, like a simple image of an old yellow farmhouse. My client could be living in the house now, or it could have been my client's childhood home, or their grandparents' house where their mother was raised. At times, I may need to ask my sitter if a particular event has happened yet, or describe a location or scene to my sitter to figure out what I'm looking at and when.

Along with intention and context, the other cue I use to understand if I'm in the past, present or future is connectedness; past and present are more strongly connected to one another and specific people than future events. Past events connect to one another and people in fairly linear ways, whereas future events feel more like a bunch of helium balloons held together on different lengths of string, sort of floating around and banging into one another as they flap in the wind. Other than their connections, there really isn't anything inherently different about past, present and future in the connected mind; they're all sort of the same.

In spiritual circles, one often hears axioms such as "There is no time" or "Time doesn't exist." Like most spiritual axioms that try and describe the infinite and timeless with words, these statements point to something real and true, but can also be misleading. You have to go beyond the simple meaning of the words, which is clearly not true, to understand the bigger meaning. Although the connected mind does seem relatively timeless, it's more accurate to say that information about the recent past, present and near future, or aspects of them, exists simultaneously in the connected mind. Some aspect of time does seem to exist in the connected mind, though it functions in less rigid and less linear ways than it does in the physical world.

People's distant futures are less accessible to me than the near future. I can see many different possible futures one big life choice out, but it's more difficult to jump two or three big life choices out into the future, suggesting to me that there is some aspect of time in the connected mind. That said, sometimes I do get future events that are way, way out, seeing people who are currently in their thirties with no children as grandparents with grandchildren, for example. I sometimes also stumble across events from the distant past, such as themes that have repeated over multiple generations related to issues that my clients are dealing with in the present for example.

The temporal equanimity of the connected mind is one reason that the connected mind is so useful: with the connected mind, it's possible to get information about the past, present and future. It's also the reason the connected mind can be so confusing and paradoxical, especially during your first few conscious experiences with it. Everything in the connected mind is sort of mushed up into one thing and it takes skill, focus and context to sort out what you are perceiving, and what it all means. For example, if I tune into You with my connected mind, I will immediately feel aspects of your essential nature. What I will see and feel is the idea of you, the essential You-ness that translates over time, something like the part of You that people can see in pictures of you at different ages. Dates and images will start flooding in with hints of associated events and experiences that illustrate how your essential nature has played out over time.

As much as that essential 'Youness' is important and central to who you are, just perceiving someone's 'Youness' without context, connections or examples of how that central essence has or is playing out in your life can be meaningless, or nonsensical. You don't always get or have context for connected mind information though, and your intention or curiosity, whatever it is you're wondering about, is often the only context you get. Some psychics will ask for a picture, or an object that belongs to someone they are trying to get information about as a way to provide context: you will get information about anything you focus on with your connected mind, starting with a picture or someone's belonging is a starting point, a way into the connected mind that narrows down the information you receive to only that which is related to the person or animal in the picture. As much as a picture or belonging can help, it's not necessary if you work by validation with a cooperative sitter to confirm and give context to the information you're getting. Simply having a client focus on a person or animal, or tell me a name or what it is they want to know is enough for me to be able to focus in on the person or animal with my connected mind.

When I see people's past experiences, most often I see things that happened routinely over time; years of experience rolled up into single scenes. For example, I will see and say things like: "Mom's in the kitchen all the time, you're chopping vegetables with your sisters, there's ten things cooking all at once, mom's the boss, everyone checks in with her to see what to do next because this place is hers and all hail to the queen." Single events do come up during my sessions but usually only events that were somehow pivotal or life changing, what I refer to as pivot points. I often only get a number associated with the scene that signifies years or months into the past, or a specific year that an event happened, and my client will need to explain what happened that changed their life to open the details of the event for me to look at.

I usually only get these single events in general and might not be able to tell if someone was 10 or 25 years old when something happened, and may only get pieces of the event, like seeing something out of the corner of your eye – I get a sense of the event but not the details. For example, I might see someone fall out of a tree and break something. Figuring out who broke what and when, why it's important, or why it's coming up in relation to a particular issue may require a joint effort. It may turn out that my client broke an arm or a leg, and came away from the experience with the belief that they can't trust themselves, or that the world is a dangerous place. Or they may have discovered that they suddenly got some much needed care and attention and subsequently continued to break themselves to get their needs met. It might turn out that their daughter fell out of the tree a month ago.

Connections come up a lot, connections between a sitter's ideas about themselves and the world, their values, beliefs and fears, and how those ideas become the seeds of repeating life experiences. As sessions progress, I tend to get a clear feel for what all my sitter's connections point to, what I refer to as *drivers* – the subtle realities behind ideas, memories, beliefs, fears and values and that affect people's lives again and again through time and effectively make us who we are. Drivers in essence are ideas that cycle through time, creating karmic loops where the same kinds of events and experiences play out over and over at multiple points throughout people's lives. Drivers also affect our bodies, health and well-being because they drive how our bodies are shaped, formed and function, how they are fueled and taken care of, as well as what we do with them.

I often tune into scenes where my sitter came to a conclusion about themselves or the world, and created a belief and associated driver. I might get an accompanying statement that links the belief to the event or scene.[21] Then I usually get ages and details about other life events where that same driver has played out, reaffirming the truth and validity of the associated belief to my sitter. I might also get possible futures where the same driver will play out again if my client does not bring consciousness to it.

In the connected mind, your ideas about yourself, your thoughts and emotions are not abstract and fleeting things that exist only in your head. They are very real nonphysical things that can be perceived and also create and flavor every aspect of your life, what happens in it, and your future. The key thing to know here is that drivers can be shaped and changed by bringing consciousness to them in the past and the present, thus altering the ways in which they ripple forward and affect the future. Simply seeing or bringing consciousness to how a driver is creating repeating patterns in your life is often enough to shift, change or stop those life patterns altogether. We can also change drivers that stem from pivotal events in our past by looking back at such events with love, understanding and acceptance and letting go of unhealthy conclusions about ourselves or the world we came to through the event.

Drivers and possible futures are just the way *I* tend to use psychic information, the way *I've* found that makes the most difference in the lives of my clients. You can take this same ability and use it in the ways that come naturally to you; ways that might not look like someone consulting you for what you can see psychically. Getting to know your telepathic side may take time but it will reveal to you how it functions best and in relation to the kind of curiosities, knowledge, talents and skills you have. The potential uses for telepathy and telepathic information are infinite, and collectively, I think humanity is just getting started with this skill and ability. I'm a neophyte who has barely scratched the surface in comparison to what future generations will be capable of. To really tap into and realize our true potentials, though, we have to stop ignoring and denying our connected minds, and realize that we live in two realities: physical reality and what I call subtle reality, and start exploring.

Subtle Realities – Whose Thought Is It Anyway?

What if it were true that nature speaks in signs and that the secret to understanding its language consists in noticing similarities in shape or in form?
~ Jeremy Narby, *The Cosmic Serpent: DNA and the Origins of Knowledge*

There is a widespread misconception in the world that something must be physical to exist; that only what can be physically touched, seen or directly measured is real. However, when connected mind adepts such as psychic-mediums, shamans or remote viewers independently focus their connected minds on the same subject, they come back with the similar or identical experiences and information.[22] The reason that multiple connected mind adepts can separately and independently focus their minds on something and experience it in the same way – much like we can all look at an object in the physical world and all see it in the same way – is that aspects of the past, present and future, as well as thoughts, thought forms, ideas, structures, places, drivers and energies exist in the connected mind, independently of any one person's mind. Such nonphysical things therefore have an objective, though nonphysical, reality.

I refer to what exists in the connected mind as *subtle realities*. Although subtle realities do have an objective existence, they exist in a way that is less objective than objects and experiences in physical reality. I refer to subtle realities as subtle because they are delicate, ephemeral and ethereal in comparison to physical reality, and are easily altered through perception alone. The very act of focusing and perceiving a subtle reality adds to its creation and shapes it, reinforcing it and making it more stable, or changing it.[23]

Objectively perceiving subtle realities requires a state of curiosity, desirelessness and non-attachment, because in the connected mind your focus follows your desire and your desire shapes what you see through the synergetic effect. When you can put aside all of your survivor mind's desires and judgements, the connected mind, and all the subtle realities in it open up. You cease seeing purely your own thought projections and accurately perceive a whole new world of authentic subtle realities as they are, not how you want them to be.

The state of curiosity, desirelessness and non-attachment required to accurately and objectively perceive subtle realities is often referred to as *being present*. I explain presence as what happens when you bring your connected mind, or authentic self, to the moment, and you perceive with your connected mind rather than with your survivor mind. Presence can also be understood as a state of unconditional love and complete nonresistance to the moment where one deeply connects with something (or someone) and perceives it as it is, imperfections and all, seeing only the perfection in the whole without the desire to change what is perceived.

In recognizing archetypes and the collective unconscious, Carl Jung began cataloguing or mapping nonphysical realities. An archetype can be defined as "universal patterns or motifs which come from the collective unconscious and are the basic content of religions, mythologies, legends, and fairy tales; emerging in individuals in the form of dreams, visions and fantasies. The archetype carries specific energies and is capable of acting upon the world."[24] Religious texts and spiritual or shamanic teachings can then also all be seen as maps or catalogues of different parts of subtle reality.

Such maps of subtle reality can be interesting, but it's important to remember that the map is not the territory and there is far, far more to any territory than a map can depict. Learning to directly perceive, navigate and work in subtle reality is far more interesting, useful and powerful than conceptually understanding subtle realities or reading about other people's experiences. Any reasonably accurate map can be useful for planning and guiding journeys to any destination, but no one can truly understand a place if they don't go there themselves. No amount of study or expertise in guides or maps can replace actually travelling and experiencing a destination for yourself either.

On any journey, if you only stick to maps and guidebooks, and never leave the resort so to speak, you'll miss out on most of what your destination has to offer. In subtle reality, you only tend to see what you are looking for and expect to find, so whatever maps you use to navigate will heavily inform your experience. For this reason, experiences in subtle reality that correlate with any particular belief system need to be taken with a grain of salt, and don't really prove that validity of any one belief system over another. Subtle reality is so vast and varied that arguing over what it is and isn't like is pointless, sort of like arguing over whether the ocean is warm or cold, cloudy or clear, full of fish or desolate, without specifying which part of the ocean you're speaking about and when. Understanding what you are experiencing and why without context and consciousness of what you are bringing to the experience is next to impossible.

The subtle realities I tend to see during my sessions range from vague hints of thoughts or ideas to vividly detailed futures and memories of past experiences played out with casts of people, buildings and landscapes that I can psychically tour and explore. When I only get a hint of a subtle reality, it's usually early on in a session as I'm getting my bearings in my sitter's subtle realities. I will know that I'm sensing a significant subtle reality, usually a pivot point, but I often only know that it is there and significant. The only information I might get about it initially is a number, age, month or year associated with the pivot point, so I will often ask simple questions like: "What happened 6 years ago... stressful event, pivotal change, or big move?"

The answer to such questions is inevitably something like: "I graduated from university", "My mom got cancer", "I met my husband" or "My house burned down". From that moment, I usually move into the details of the subtle reality of the event, sharing what happened, the relationship dynamics or beliefs at play, and what conclusion my sitter came to about themselves through the event. I will then usually get other ages or years that are connected to the same belief or subtle reality to help my sitter connect the dots of their own life themes. When I tune into one significant life event, I will then often see other events, choices, issues or people in my sitter's life connected to the event, and the driver behind all the events – the thought, belief, energy or fear that is continuing to play out in my sitter's thoughts, mood, relationships, health, career, finances and life events.

When I work with people over the course of several years, I inevitably see some of the same subtle realities and subsequently bring up some of the same information each time, even if I have no recollection of the person or our prior sessions, or if I'm reading someone who is connected to another client I have read. In other words, I consistently see the same subtle realities in association with the same people: "Yes, you mentioned that in our last session" or "That came up in my mom's session". I know I'm not remembering or making logical associations because I don't remember most of my sessions, or even the people I've read. I mostly work by phone, so I hardly ever have a face to match to a name. I actually have to ask most people I work with if I've read them before.

When I work, I quite literally put my thinking mind aside to do the work of translating subtle realities. I don't do deep trance work, and I am always fully conscious in the moment, able to analyze and contextualize information after I've found it. My memory just doesn't want to hold onto the information I've translated after the fact. The further into connection I go, the more single pointed my focus, the more fully I lose myself in the process and what I am focusing on, the less I remember, even in the moment. When I'm translating subtle realities for someone else, it's not my job to remember, just to experience and translate. Looking at other people's subtle realities is sort of like looking at other people's memories in that they're not mine, so I don't need to remember them and therefore choose not to. I imagine that my life would be very stressful and confusing if I remembered all of my client's subtle realities. Having other people's memories in my head wouldn't leave much space for me.

I think it's hard for people to understand how I can share intimate and emotional moments with them, along with detailed accounts of places, people and events, and a month (sometimes moments) later, have no recollection of the content of the session, or sometimes even that we've had one. It's not personal, and it doesn't mean that such moments weren't genuine. Just the opposite. I've even done this with my husband, sharing insights into the dynamic of our marriage with him in a deeply connected state, overwhelmed with emotion, and then having little memory of the session days later. When I'm reminded, I can go back and look at the same subtle realities, and I often get the sense that I've seen them before, a sort of déjà vu, but I never have the sense that I am bringing them up from memory. It's more like returning to a place I've been before, remembering having been there but still having to look around to take in the details of the place.

The concept of subtle realities can be very paradoxical, even disturbing at first. We aren't used to thinking of thoughts as having anything other than a transient, separate, private and inconsequential existence inside the boundaries of our own heads. Most of us understand thought only as the voice in our head, our imagination, or the daydreaming we indulge in from time to time. We assume our thoughts are our own creation, and only come from and exist within our brains. Our thoughts seem to flash into our minds, then completely disappear as if they never existed. When we say that we are 'thinking about' something, it's assumed that we are focusing on our own mind's conception of whatever it is we are thinking about, and that every thought we have comes from within our own brains, then evaporates. When we focus in our imagination or our survivor minds, we *are* using our brains, and focusing on our own tiny constructed realities – the world as our lives have taught us it is, and how we think it should be. With our connected mind, which is not contained within our brains, none of our usual presumptions apply.

The notion that when we think about something, if we tune into its subtle reality, we are actually observing something real, that other people can also observe, and that we shape what we observe through the mere act of observing it, can be a lot to take in. If you spend some time noticing the qualities of your thoughts, however, you will notice that some thoughts come to mind quicker and easier than others. Some sensory thoughts come to mind very easily in great detail, whereas others are blurry, with only enough detail to get a sense of the thought – like a blob of mercury on a table that shifts out from under you whenever you try to put your finger in it – no matter what you do, you can't pin it down.

If you consistently imagine the same people, places, or things, you will also notice your imaginings get easier each time, and what you are imagining becomes brighter, more detailed, more stable over time, and easier to pin down each time – like a well-worn groove on a record. Imagine the same person or thing again and again over time, and the speed and ease with which the picture pops into your head each time may start to give you a sense that what you are imagining actually exists; that you're observing, not remembering or imagining anymore. If you can accomplish this, you will know that it's not just your imagination, you have created[25] or established a connection to a subtle reality;

something that doesn't just exist within the confines of your own mind, something that can affect others and physical reality, and something that others with sufficient connected mind ability can perceive.

If you create or connect to a subtle reality as an exercise, by meditating daily for example and repeatedly focusing on a person, place, thing, theme or scenario in sensory detail, you will undoubtedly find that subtle reality showing up in your life, somehow, somewhere. For example, if you decide to focus on a yellow Volkswagen Bug in meditation daily, your thought of the yellow Volkswagen Bug will eventually become a potent subtle reality, or your thought will attach you to a potent subtle reality related to yellow cars, Volkswagens and Bugs. You will find that your attention is continually brought to yellow cars, Volkswagens, and yellow Volkswagen Bugs in particular as you drive around in the physical world. This can partly be attributed to your brain simply noticing the yellow cars and Volkswagens that are already out there, but if you carefully notice your noticing, you will likely find that you are not just noticing; your actions are also being inspired.

You might find yourself inexplicably looking in a particular direction just as a yellow Volkswagen Bug drives by, as if part of you knew it was going to be there before it came into view. You may also find yourself driving routes that you wouldn't ordinarily take, going places for seemingly random reasons, or choosing to watch particular movies, and find that having done so, you inexplicably come across yellow Volkswagen Bugs somehow. You may even find that people randomly bring up Volkswagen Bugs in conversations, post pictures on Facebook or bring the theme of the subtle reality into your life in some way. A friend might even suddenly decide to buy a yellow Volkswagen, invite you to a dinner party where another guest owns a Volkswagen Bug, or you might get in a fender-bender with one.

Subtle realities show up in life and shape your experience of physical reality in very strange and often entirely unpredictable ways, illustrating the strange and far-reaching ways everything is connected through subtle reality. This exercise can be done with any object, thought or idea to familiarize yourself with the strange ways subtle realities can manifest and play out in life, and prove to yourself just how powerful your connected mind is. I suggested picking an enjoyable subtle reality to bring into your life though. You can also use this exercise, and understanding of subtle reality, to create your day by meditating on a specific feeling or idea each morning, such as appreciation or love. Whatever you meditate on consistently with vivid sensory detail will eventually show up in your life somehow, often in unexpectedly delightful ways. Meditating or focusing on anything with a sense of resistance or lack or on the absence of something is equally effective so be mindful of the energy you focus with, as well as what you choose to focus on.

To give you an example of the strange and far-reaching ways drivers and subtle realities can play out, I'll share what happened on a retreat I recently attended. A friend of mine, who I had attended several retreats with before at various locations around Ontario and New York State, was shocked when he arrived at the new retreat location: the one-room schoolhouse he had briefly attended primary school in, forty years prior. The property had been purchased and turned into a retreat center; however, the one-room schoolhouse was just as it was in his youth.

My friend had been raised Mennonite, and never quite felt that he fit in at school. During primary school, he was regularly in trouble for not sitting still, or saying the wrong thing in class, and had regularly been sent to sit outside the classroom as punishment. When our retreat started, everyone found a space on the floor in the building where they could meditate, stretch out and lie down for an extended period. The retreat facilitator quickly recognized that there wasn't quite enough space in the classroom and asked my friend (specifically) to please move his spot out to the hall. My friend complied, and realized with shock and dismay when he got to the hall that he had, yet again, been sent to sit out in the hall.

The patterns of our lives repeat in strange and unexpected ways. Understanding and bringing conscious awareness to the drivers and triggers that create these patterns can transform them from painful loops that reaffirm beliefs like "I'm bad and I don't fit in", towards life affirming, joyful and fulfilling patterns that fill in around drivers related to beliefs like "I'm unique and the world celebrates and accommodates my uniqueness."

Of course, sometimes it's difficult to tell if you chose to focus on a subtle reality, and brought an event into your physical reality, or if you happened to pick up on a potent subtle reality that was already strong enough to play out in the physical world. For example, if you find yourself thinking of an old friend and suddenly they call you out of the blue, it might seem like you caused your friend to call you by focusing on him or her. It might also seem like you intuited your friend's call; that your friend's future call caused you to think about them in the past. Your friend might be calling you because they had an accident, a great success, or perhaps got sick, in which case it may seem like your thoughts had been brought to your old friend because of your emotional connection and a potent change in your friend's subtle reality. Cause and effect are sometimes very hard to pick apart; in fact, cause and effect can be nonsensical concepts to try and apply to subtle realities, which exist outside of time. It's more accurate to think of your thoughts about your friend before him calling you, and his calling you, as having been orchestrated in subtle reality, outside of time, and both events as being the effects of a single shared subtle reality – a single event.

The realization some may find interesting, others disturbing, is that we all have connected mind abilities whether we are aware of them or not, and it is difficult, even when you are quite adept with your connected mind, to discern between your own thoughts versus someone else's subtle realities. The whole concept of ownership (of who a thought or a subtle reality belongs to) becomes rather meaningless once a thought becomes a subtle reality, is perceived by more than one person, and takes on its own independent existence in the connected mind. What is important to understand is that although subtle realities can be created through sensory thought or imagining, they are the subject thought of, not thoughts in and of themselves. Though we might say that we are having a thought when we focus on a subtle reality, and in a sense we are, the thought isn't necessarily our own. What we are focusing our thought on might be much more than what we ordinarily think of as a thought.

I've had many experiences, perhaps you have as well, where I've been minding my own business, picking out produce in a grocery store for example, and out of nowhere, suddenly having been hijacked by strange thoughts – images, ideas or feelings that are completely out of character or have nothing to do with me. I often ask the question out loud, "Why am I thinking about..." Sometimes the answer is straightforward and whoever I'm with will explain that I had tuned into something that was bothering them, they were thinking about, or had just happened. Other times, there is no apparent answer to the question of "Why am I thinking about...", or there are no clear images, just anxiety and fear-filled thoughts disguised as my own. It's still sometimes hard for me to remember in the moment that such thoughts and anxieties aren't necessarily mine, that I can examine the thought and sometimes follow it to a source outside of myself, sometimes a fellow shopper down the aisle.

Separating what thoughts and feelings belong to who can be tricky though. I may have my own worries that resonate with a fellow shopper's anxious state, and my survivor mind might bring up all kinds of resonate thought scenarios that I could get lost in. It took a long time for me to get it, but once I could remember in such moments that I was in a peaceful happy state only moments before, and understood that I had momentarily mistaken someone else's energetic state for my own, it became really simple to snap out of other people's energy. If I find myself suddenly affected by someone else's stress, I now try to come back to the truth that I am peaceful and happy, and recall or find new thoughts to get lost in as a way to alter my state into one of my choosing. That is how we control our experience and create our own reality; we choose what we focus on, and in so doing, the subtle realities that will manifest in our lives.

Learning to discern the difference between having one's own thoughts, thought energies that are influencing you, and focusing on something outside of oneself that is made out of thought energy is a key connected mind skill. Having a daily meditation practice, where you practice getting into or snapping back to a peaceful, blank state, from which you can objectively look at any thoughts you are having, or that are being impressed upon you, can be very helpful in this regard. The trap many budding telepaths fall into when they first open up is believing that every perception that crosses their mind has meaning, is a sign, a warning or a vision of an impending calamity. Please relax! It's easy to drive yourself and others crazy when you first become receptive to subtle realities if you insist that every perception that crosses your mind has meaning or on scaring everyone. Calm objectivity along with the intention and ability to just watch your thoughts and perceptions, along with firm boundaries about what you are willing to look at and when is essential if you're going to start exploring subtle reality.

Playing in Subtle Reality… Spontaneous Knowing and Telepathic Networks

The restraint of the modifications of the mind-stuff is Yoga.

Then the seer (self) abides in his own true nature…

By Cultivating attitudes of friendliness toward the happy, compassion for the unhappy, delight in the virtuous, and disregard for the wicked, the mindstuff remains in undisturbed calmness.

Or that calm is retained by the controlled exhalation or retention of breath.

Or by meditating on anything one chooses that is elevating.

Or the concentration on subtle sense perceptions can cause steadiness of mind…

Gradually, one's mastery in concentration extends from the primal atom to the greatest magnitude.

~ *The Yoga Sutras of Pantanjali* translated by Sri Swami Satchidananda

Some subtle realities are relatively clear and easy to perceive; they are stable, detailed and bright. Others can be very delicate, ethereal, and are easily distorted by any projected idea or desire. I use the term *potency* to refer to the stability, detail and brightness of subtle realities. In general, subtle realities are made more potent the more time is spent focusing on them, the more intently they are focused on, the more emotion they are focused on with, and the more people focus on them. Potency is also a measure of the degree to which subtle realities influence physical reality, and the likelihood of a subtle reality becoming a physical reality.

Subtle realities are dynamic blueprints for physical reality, creating and influencing the shapes and forms of the physical world, and what happens in it. You can think of subtle realities as shadows of physical reality through time, and physical reality as a projection of subtle reality around which physical matter forms. So tuning into the subtle reality of an acorn, you will perceive the oak tree it will become, and vice versa. You might also perceive a misshapen limb and the storm that will cause the limb to break, the birds and children that will frequent the tree, or the rhythm of the seasons.

Single survivor mind thoughts such as "I think I'll go to the movies tonight" are not very potent and, so, are difficult to perceive objectively. You might say they are barely real, in the subtle sense of the word. This makes telepathy, in the conventional sense where a telepath hears or reads the thoughts crossing another person's mind, very difficult, except when someone happens to be focusing on a very potent subtle reality. The thought "I think I'll go to the movies tonight" has no potency, but if you imagine going to the movies in sensory detail, taste the popcorn, feel the seat, re-experience the thrills of a suspenseful movie you've seen, or maybe relive a great kiss at the drive-in, you're focusing on some potent subtle realities you've connected to the movies – potent subtle realities other people can pick up on.

I don't spend much time focusing on perceiving what most people are thinking in any given moment, but I easily perceive changes in people's state or energy as different thoughts cross their minds. With intent and focus, I can often get a sense of the thoughts crossing people's minds and what they are connected to, especially if they happen to be potent thoughts that are emotionally charged, or thoughts that someone has focused on repeatedly. I don't, however, wander about the world reading people's thoughts as I don't think it's ethical, or even interesting, let alone enjoyable. The fear of having one's thoughts read does seem to be rather widespread though, as many people I meet outside of a work context actually gasp and ask me if I'm reading their thoughts or know their secrets when they find out I'm telepathic.

I would like to reassure everyone that I don't believe there is any cause for concern in regard to having your thoughts read, and dark secrets judged or outed. Just for the record, your dark secrets, all the things you are deeply ashamed of and hide, when you lump them all together with everyone else's, are not a big deal, nothing to be ashamed of, and are likely pretty commonplace. You might be shocked by the things that I see and hear during any given workday. It all gets really normal. I've seen and heard so much, held space for so many people as they face and heal their traumas, shames and secrets that it's impossible for me to judge anybody, let alone seek out more of the same when I'm not working. I've always said, I have a deep admiration and respect for my clients; I think they are courageous and badass because they are all so willing to face their stories and open up to growing in new ways to move forward. They remind me every day that I am surrounded by an evolving consciousness striving for its own betterment.

States of judgement or fear, any ideas based in separateness, keep you out of your connected mind, so it isn't really even possible to accurately read someone else's thoughts from a place of judgement, fear, manipulation or ill intent. Even if a telepath were to start out trying to get information by reading someone's thoughts from a place of judgement or ill intent, such feelings are likely to disappear once the telepath comes into connection. It's hard not to fall in love with what you connect with on a deep level, and it is very hard to judge or harm what you love.

What is mostly likely to happen when a telepath comes from a place of fear, negativity or ill intent is that the negativity will warp the telepath's perceptions, and the telepath will only see resonantly negative portions of a person's subtle realities and their own projections, rendering the information they get useless, or even harmful, even if there is a grain of truth to it. Unfortunately, I think this happens all too frequently with some people who are psychic enough to get some information, but haven't done their personal growth work, and project their own fears and negativity into their readings and telepathic perception of the world; one of the major reasons I always tell people to choose a psychic, medium or telepath through referral only.

I have spent a fair amount of time in my work helping people recover from bad experiences with psychics who were skilled enough to pick up on clients' fears, but not much else. Just because a psychic can pick up on a few themes relevant to your life doesn't mean that you should listen to them or that they are a skilled psychic. I've met clients who had been told by psychics that they had a stalker, that their husband was going to have a bad accident, and worse. These fears never came to pass for these people, and the ominous predictions were not possible futures that I could pick up on when I read these clients, only unresolved worries and fears. Sadly, these psychics did nothing more than scare these people and, in doing so, increased the likelihood of their fears actually coming to pass by scaring them into focusing on negative outcomes and putting them in states of stress. Totally unacceptable!

Getting some psychic information right sometimes is a dangerous thing if you are not aware of how the questions you ask, along with your own baggage and fears, can warp the information you receive. If you do receive anything other than empowering information from a psychic, or get anything other than empowering information if you are working with your own abilities, please carefully consider the source and the questions being asked. If you do have worries or fears that you want psychic information about, ask empowering, solution oriented questions like, "How can I make sure I'm safe on this trip?", a question that may yield usable information to keep you safe, not "Do you see any danger in my future", a question that will have an answer, and will cause you to focus on fear and negativity, and increase the likelihood of something bad actually happening.

Although I don't read people's thoughts in the moment out in the world, or as part of my regular work, I do occasionally use telepathy in the moment when I work with athletes. For example, telepathically reading a golfer as they approach a ball and during their swing, I can perceive the various thoughts crossing their mind, and the effect it is having on their energy, power, swing, focus and the overall outcome of the shot. I can usually pick out the thought that came up during a shot, why it came up, and what else the thought is connected to. Dissecting exactly what happened afterwards requires a joint effort and gives golfers who are already technically proficient an opportunity to perfect their mental game.

I have also used telepathy with athletes to improve their ability to get into and stay in *the zone*. Athletes know the connected mind very well. The zone is that place where:

- time seems to slow down and you perceive things in slow motion;
- you perceive everything and everybody on the field or court at once, simultaneously, including what's happening, what everyone is doing, where the play or ball is going and how elements such as wind or ground conditions are affecting the play;
- your actions synchronize with other players as if you are telepathically connected (you are);
- your body acts and reacts pre-cognitively, knowing exactly what to do, where to be and when, before you can think about it or have any conscious awareness of why you are moving or acting, as if part of you knows what's going to happen before it happens (part of you does).

In other words, the zone describes a synergy of connected mind skills applied directly to the moment; skills that can be broken down, practiced, strengthened and honed off the field to improve performance on the field. Creative visualization has become the norm for world-class athletes for good reason, even if very few people understand how and why it works so well.

'Zone skills' can also be brought from the field into real life. Great athletes are gifted telepaths. They know their connected mind very well from time spent running, swimming, practicing or playing. Incidentally, I think our deep cultural obsession with sports and performance, both artistic and competitive, can be understood in somewhat spiritual terms: when we witness a perfect play or outstanding performance, we are witnessing people in deep connection bringing the poignancy of their connected mind into physical reality through mediums like movement and sound. It's no wonder we are so culturally obsessed with sports and art, and so moved by great performances: they remind us of who we really are and what we are really capable of when we are completely connected and expressing our full potential.

Though most individual language-based thoughts like "I have to go to the store" have almost no potency and are very difficult to perceive telepathically, thoughts that are repeatedly returned to become more potent and easier to objectively perceive. They become more real; stable subtle realities that exist in the connected mind that can be revisited, not just by you but by others as well. Ideas and thoughts that are shared or focused on by many become very potent, more real still, and even easier to perceive. Many of your thoughts in any given day, or minute for that matter, are not your own. Your connected mind is always there, always on, and always connected. Many thoughts that pop into your head, which might be dismissed as random, are not random at all. They are not your personal thoughts. Rather, your connected mind has tuned into a potent subtle reality, or someone has impressed a thought on you by focusing on you.

Just by focusing or thinking about someone, you open a telepathic connection with them, or widen an existing one.

Whatever your state or predominant thought when you open this connection will be shared and impressed upon the person you're focusing on. This is why it's important to ground yourself in connection daily, and in thoughts of peace, appreciation and cooperation, especially if you have to deal with workplaces or environments that are filled with toxic people and telepathic chatter. You not only immunize yourself against the influence of toxic telepathic chatter, you also influence and calm the telepathic environment around you through subtle reality. Connection works both ways! Just don't start thinking that you can permanently transform a toxic environment all by yourself purely through love and connection though; the energy drain of such endeavors is enormous. You will more likely 'vibrate yourself out' of such environments by getting synchronistically reassigned, promoted or kicked out the door before you can affect permanent change anyway.

Most people's day to day language-based thoughts are not potent enough for even skilled telepaths to perceive, but many sensory-emotional thoughts are potent enough that anyone in the vicinity, or connected to the person having the thought, can feel or perceive it. Many subtle realities are also potent enough to be spontaneously picked up and perceived by many people's connected minds, no matter how skilled. Some subtle realities are potent enough, or suddenly become potent enough, to spontaneously enter many people's awareness, regardless of their connected mind ability. Spontaneous awareness of subtle realities can happen in a few ways, through potency alone, or through a combination of potency and focus, proximity or connection.

Any event, positive or negative, that captures the simultaneous attention of many people has a correspondingly potent subtle reality that can be felt before and after the event, or at a distance during the event by anyone that is somehow connected to the event. Events that are shared or witnessed by large numbers of people and have a high emotional impact have correspondingly potent subtle realities. I think it's for this reason that premonitions of impending disasters by ordinary people are rather common, along with an abundance of reports of near misses where people narrowly escape death by just missing their boarding call or cancelling their seat on a doomed flight for example, seemingly by chance.

Obviously animals also have connected minds, and mostly live in their connected minds, pick up on subtle realities easily, and have regularly been reported to act strangely prior to earthquakes and other such events that influence hundreds or thousands of people with correspondingly potent subtle realities. Signatures of potent subtle realities, or potent changes in subtle reality, have also been detected by scientists. For example, in the Global Consciousness Project, an experiment started in 1998 directed by Princeton scientist Roger Neilson. The project has documented simultaneous changes in the randomness of random number generators stationed around the world prior to major world events. The most significant change in randomness detected to date was documented on September 11, 2001, and started five hours prior to the first plane hitting the World Trade Center.

Focus is probably the most common way people spontaneously become aware of subtle realities, either because they inadvertently focus on a subtle reality they have picked up on by letting their mind wander, or by being focused on by someone else. People's ability to sense when they are being stared at has been well documented by biologist Rupert Sheldrake in numerous studies. Intently thinking about someone has a similar effect, and you have experienced instances in your own life where someone has called you out of the blue, seemingly for no reason, just after you were intently thinking about them. You may also have noticed the surprising frequency with which people say: "Hey! I was just thinking about you!" when they run into someone they haven't seen in awhile or, "Your ears must be burning, we were just talking about you." You may even remember thinking, "Hey! I was just singing that song in my head" when a particular song was played on the radio. When you let your mind wander, or a thought suddenly pops into your head, you're doing more than just daydreaming.

Subtle realities can be connected to particular locations, and can be so potent that you feel them well before you enter a space. Lots of people have had the experience of a space giving them the creeps or making them feel light, festive and bubbly. Sacred places, historic sites, slaughterhouses, sports stadiums, schools and hospitals all have potent subtle realities, where the energy of what happens in the space, and past events connected to the space, is imbued into the space and can be felt long after the events have taken place. Subtle realities related to specific events and people can absolutely be connected to specific places. Such is the case with many so-called hauntings, where a very potent subtle reality connected to a traumatic event can be felt by almost anyone entering that space. In such cases, people with connected mind skill can tune into the subtle reality to discover the events that created the energy signature.

The strange thing about energy signatures is that subtle realities tend to play out repeatedly in loops, and anyone in a space that has a heavy energy signature will be affected by the subtle reality of the space. People who live in, spend time in or are deeply connected with a haunted space may unconsciously play out the subtle realities connected to the space. This gives rise to what I think is a reasonable and legitimate fear of haunted places, as well as a sound reason for energy clearings. For example, there was a bar in my hometown where a number people were murdered over the years. Casual observation would suggest that it was just that kind of bar, where the kind of people who murder other people hang out. The odd thing was, this bar had largely become a student bar, and students aren't usually known for their murderous ways. The bar was eventually torn down, and a luxury apartment building built on the site a few years later. Despite the change in the land use and clean up, the site still managed to attract several stabbings and a shooting in the years after the bar was gone in spite of the site's total makeover.

On the positive side, you can intentionally tune into, use and benefit from subtle realities associated with spaces such as temples, libraries or gyms to positively affect your behavior or results towards productive ends. Any space that is created for a specific purpose, or repeatedly used for a specific purpose, will have an energy signature and associated subtle reality to match. Simply by being in a space such as a university, gym, library or temple, you will be affected by the energy of the space, and will find studying easier and more productive in a library, or meditation easier and deeper in a temple, provided you align yourself with the subtle reality of the space by using it for its intended purpose. By repeatedly visiting such spaces, you can imbue yourself with the energy of the space, essentially 'downloading' information attached to the space into your subtle reality: the subtle reality of the space becomes part of your subtle reality, a driver that will repeatedly play out in your life. By repeatedly visiting a space, you will also affect the space; what you do in that space, and what you bring to the space becomes *synergetically* connected to the subtle reality of the space.

Synergy refers to the idea that elements of a system work together to become more than the sum of their parts, and the presence or absence of one or more elements, however big or small, can profoundly affect the whole system. Subtle reality is highly synergetic, and the energy of a space can change dramatically through the synergetic absence, presence or connection of a single person from that space. Such is often the case with restaurants, where food can suddenly go from being wonderful to awful or vice versa, even though the recipes, ingredients and staff may not have changed. A change in ownership, management, or the absence or presence of a single cook or chef can profoundly affect the energy and flavor of everything in a restaurant, even if nothing else has changed. You can often feel a single person's presence or absence in a company, space or organization. Similarly, we may notice the synergetic presence, or absence, of people in our own lives: when everything is different when someone is around, in your life, or no longer in your life, you are feeling the person's synergetic influence, or lack thereof, in your life.

Spontaneous awareness of subtle realities can also occur through your personal connections. Your connected mind is more sensitive to people, places and animals that you are connected to somehow. Love is probably the strongest measure of connection, but by no means the only one. Mother's intuition and the often-reported phenomenon of one twin feeling another twin's pain are well-known examples of spontaneous awareness of subtle realities through connection. Twins that were separated at birth, and reunited later offer a fascinating glimpse into the influence of deep connection and shared subtle realities. Separated twins have been studied quite thoroughly by scientists[26] and the results reported in the news regularly over the years. Most journalists and scientists tend to discuss the findings of such studies in terms of nature versus nurture, attributing the astounding similarities and coincidences between the lives of separated twins solely to genetics.

Many of the so-called coincidences, however, defy any material explanation. Coincidences like one set of twins having been given the same names by their adopting families, both marrying women with the same first name, both twins giving their sons the same first and middle names, and both twins owning dogs with the same names. Other sets of twins were found to both smoke the same brand of cigarettes, drive the same models of cars, and vacation in the same destinations, without ever having met one another. I find it entertaining that logical, educated people can still somehow attribute such strikingly improbable synchronicities to genetics without suggesting any sort of mechanism to explain how shared DNA can translate into twins marrying wives with the same names, let alone twins being given the same name by different sets of adopting parents. Those are some potent genes!

Indirect connections, like your friends' friends' friends, also permit spontaneous awareness of other people's subtle realities, spontaneous awareness that affects us on a very deep level. I look to the fascinating work scientists have done exploring social networks to illustrate how subtle realities are shared between indirectly connected people – one of the many cases where scientists have investigated and documented telepathic phenomena without necessarily realizing they have done so. The subject is thoroughly discussed in the book *Connected: The Surprising Power of Our Social Networks and How They Shape Our Lives – How Your Friends' Friends' Friends Affect Everything You Feel, Think, and Do* by Nicholas A. Christakis and James H. Fowler. The title of the book is self-explanatory: the science of social networks shows that everything you feel, think and do is affected by everyone you are connected to, and that *you* affect everyone you are connected to.

If you are healthy and fit, your friends, their friends, and their friends, are all also significantly more likely to be healthy and fit, and vice versa, even though you may not know or ever meet any of the people who affect you and you affect in return. The same goes for political views, fashion choices, income levels – you name it. We are reflections of our social networks and vice versa, deeply connected and profoundly influenced by our communities, no matter how individual or separate we believe we are. The authors of *Connected* don't delve into the topic of how the deep connectedness they have documented comes about, only briefly suggesting that the mechanisms such as unconscious mimicry, emotional contagion and conversational/visual information transfer may be responsible. From a telepath's point of view, these proposed mechanisms are actually the effects of spontaneous awareness through shared subtle realities, not the cause.

In my view, the deep connectedness that shows up in many areas of science is clear evidence that we are connected to one another through more than just physical material means, on a deeper level, through subtle reality and the connected mind. This deep connection has actually been showing up in every area of science and medicine for a very long time, and science is much further ahead in understanding telepathy and subtle reality than it may outwardly appear. There is already a lot of science out there that tells us how subtle realities function, even though it was not intended to do so. For example, in *Connected*, Christakis and Fowler explain how their research, and the work of other scholars, shows that the spread of influence in a social network obeys what they call the *three degrees of influence rule*, saying: "everything we do or say tends to ripple through our network, having an impact on our friends (one degree), our friends' friends (two degrees), and even our friends' friends' friends (three degrees). Our influence gradually dissipates and ceases to have a noticeable effect on people beyond the social frontier that lies at three degrees of separation. Likewise, we are influenced by friends within three degrees but generally not by those beyond. The Three Degrees Rule applies to a broad range of attitudes, feelings and behaviors, and it applies to the spread of phenomena as diverse as political views, weight gain, and happiness."[27]

If we are all telepathically connected to one another, and share part of our minds with one another, the three degrees rule tells us a little bit about who we share our minds with and how subtle reality functions. Christakis and Fowler's rules for life in a network are:

- We shape our network.
- Our network shapes us.
- Our friends affect us, and we affect them.
- Our friends' friends affect us, and we affect them.
- Our friends' friends' friends affect us, and us them.
- The network has a life of its own.

Restated to acknowledge our telepathic connection to our social networks, and that part of each of us, our connected minds, exists and interacts with telepathic networks through subtle reality, we might say:

- We shape subtle reality.
- Subtle realities shape us.
- Our subtle realities are strongly shared within three degrees.
- Subtle realities have a life of their own.

My conjecture is that in documenting the dynamics of social networks in *Connected,* Christakis and Fowler have revealed a spiritual understanding of the world that has been known for millennia, and contextualized it in modern terms. Mapped out geometrically with circles, the three degrees rule has a curious and uncanny similarity to the flower of life: an ancient symbol that has appeared across the world in many traditions over several millennia. The symbol is said to depict a type of akashic record of basic information of all living things, to contain the fundamental forms of all matter, space and time, and to be the visual expression of the connections of life that run through all sentient beings.

I often see my clients' telepathic networks, the people who they share their minds with, reveal themselves, along with the profound and strange effects of shifts in subtle reality which can be created when my clients firmly decide to change their thinking, or courageously decide to make a life change. As a result of a seemingly tiny decision, a simple shift in their thinking, or a change in a client's conception of who they are and what they deserve, I regularly watch many of my clients' entire lives dramatically change, all on their own. Sometimes work opportunities, friends and communities emerge out of nowhere, as if by pure chance. Other times, my clients inexplicably lose friends, sometimes family, even jobs and houses, usually through no fault or conscious action of their own. Their entire life transforms because they have changed their mind and cut themselves off from or tuned out of the subtle realities and people that were not serving them. It's sort of like they get kicked out of their old life because they no longer resonate with any of the people or subtle realities they once did.

Although such dramatic shifts can be difficult, the people who take them on often see their health improve, nagging issues disappear, and old habits that they struggled to break suddenly go away – they truly become new people by choosing who they want to be and not being who they are because of the circumstances and people that happened to befall them in life. They now resonate with an entirely new set of subtle realities, and their bodies, relationships, fashion, habits, mannerisms, vocabulary and finances often transform as a result. Their minds are often cleaner, clearer and calmer, because they have tuned out of the toxic telepathic chatter that their old telepathic network exposed them to. In such cases new friends, opportunities and careers that are more in tune with their new mindset show up, though sometimes not as quickly as they would like. Transforming your life and being true to your authentic self is not always easy, but it doesn't have to be hard and it can certainly be deliciously enjoyable and cathartic.

In many cases, rather than lose friends and family who won't change, I see courageous participants accept themselves, be who they really want to be, and transform their friends and families in the process. These people are met with acceptance and respect (often after initial resistance) when they make life changes, and often inspire or telepathically influence their friends and family to make positive changes themselves. As Marianne Williamson and Nelson Mandela have famously said, "When let you your own light shine, you unconsciously give others permission to do the same."

I sometimes also see the reverse effects of these subtle reality flips as well, with much needless frustration: many people find themselves going back to old habits, having old issues rearing their ugly head, or behaving in unexpected or strange ways when they go home for the holidays, move, or reacquaint themselves with an old friend. There's no need to get frustrated or alarmed. We simply tend to play out the subtle realities we're exposed to, or focus on; we revert to that which binds us; how we used to connect. When we recognize that we share our minds, understand how we share our minds, and with whom, we empower ourselves to be entertained rather than upset or disturbed while we watch unwanted ideas and thoughts cross our minds; the source of many of our thoughts and impulses is not necessarily *us*. The solution to unwanted thoughts, ideas and impulses showing up is simply having good boundaries by changing our focus and tuning in to preferred, chosen people and subtle realities, not worrying about the constant invitations we have around us to tune into and play out displeasing or unwanted subtle realities.

Another objective understanding of the dynamics of subtle reality and personal telepathic networks comes from anthropologist Robin Dunbar. Dunbar correlated average primate brain size to average social group size and, based on the average size of the human brain, extrapolated the maximum number of people with whom human beings can maintain stable social relationships to be around 150.[28] This number has turned out to be uncannily important in business, military strategy and sociology, and has repeatedly turned up in the study of seemingly unrelated subjects such as the spread of trends, disease and even suicides.

Militaries, corporations, and many communities have historically tended to self-organize into groups of about 150 people. Groups of less than 150 people tend to work as a cohesive unit, any more than 150 people in a group and communication and cohesiveness breaks down. The approximate number of 150, referred to as Dunbar's number, turns out to be the maximum number of people that can cohesively work or live together: information, ideas and behaviors travel quickly through groups of around 150 people or less.

Dunbar's number along with its importance in the mechanics of trends is explored by Malcolm Gladwell in *The Tipping Point*, another mainstream work that we think explores the mechanics and effects of telepathic connections without touching on the idea that we are all telepathically connected. In *The Tipping Point*, Gladwell takes on a topic that has defied most conventional analysis and logical understanding: the spread of trends. He explains that a tipping point must be reached for any idea, behavior, trend, virus or disease to become widespread. The spread, or failure to spread, of everything from fashion, to rumors, to syphilis, to crime, to smoking, to social norms, to suicides, to the popularity of TV shows and books follows the tipping point pattern.

Gladwell gives us three factors that determine if something will reach a tipping point and spread: the law of the few, stickiness and context. The law of the few tells us that a few key people are needed or are responsible for the spread of any trend:

a few people who are either connected across different communities, or who are influential, either through charisma or the desire to help others make better decisions. Stickiness explains that for an idea to spread, it must be sticky. It must stick in the minds of people who are exposed to it so that they return to the idea again, repeat it or play it out. Context is the flip side to stickiness. In order for an idea to spread, the population through which a trend spreads must be receptive to a new idea, or exposed to the idea within a context that makes the idea sticky.

Gladwell gives the strange example of crime in New York City to illustrate stickiness and context. Violent crime was rampant in New York City through the 1980s and deterrents like tougher enforcement, vigilantism and harsher punishments had little effect. A rapid decline in violent crime was, however, achieved during the 1990s based on the broken windows theory – the idea that subtle signs of deterioration in a neighborhood, like broken windows, could lead to major changes in behavior of residents and declines in the quality of living. By painting over graffiti daily, fixing broken windows, and enforcing minor laws against things such as public urination and jumping subway turnstiles without paying fares, New York City eliminated the context in which ideas like 'times are hard, you need to steal and kill to survive, it's every man for himself' were sticky and spread easily, and created a context in which ideas related to community, safety and peaceful cohabitation could take hold. In doing so, New York City completed what is probably the largest Feng Shui makeover in history and transformed itself from being one of the most dangerous places in the world to one of the safest.

In terms of subtle reality, we suggest that tipping points are reached when subtle realities reach a level of potency where they can be easily picked up on telepathically by many people, and are then subconsciously played out across interconnected telepathic networks. Our subtle realities drive our behaviors and how we behave is a reflection of the subtle realities we are tuned into and connected to. The way in which trends spread reveals to whom and to what degree people are telepathically connected, in essence who people share their minds with.

For a subtle reality or trend to spread across populations, people who don't necessarily belong to any one particular community but who are connected to, or can connect to, many communities are essential. Malcolm Gladwell refers to such people as connectors, salesmen or mavens. We would explain connectors in terms of focus: anyone can become a connector, and telepathically connect large numbers of people to particular subtle realities when they draw the attention and focus of many people, whether through existing connections, celebrity, office, deed, virtue or notoriety.

Rather than stickiness and context, we suggest the idea of resonance: we tend to pick up on and play out subtle realities that resonate or fit with our image of ourselves and our existing subtle realities. The concept of resonance comes from physics and music, where vibrating objects, such as strings on an instrument, easily absorb and transmit energy at specific frequencies, and not others. Strum a well-tuned guitar string in a room full of well-tuned guitars and every other guitar string of the same note in the room will absorb some of the sound energy produced and vibrate in unison with the guitar you strummed. Out of tune guitar strings won't resonate, and won't absorb any of the sound energy you've produced; however, other instruments in the room that are tuned to the sound frequencies you produced by strumming the guitar, and harmonics of those frequencies, will resonate, and absorb the sound energy from the guitar you strummed too.

The workings of the entire physical world can largely be understood through the idea of resonance as all subatomic particles, atoms, molecules and substances absorb and transmit energy only at particular frequencies, and in particular amounts of energy called quanta – which is where the term quantum physics originates. The entire dance of physical reality, all of the interactions, exchanges and transformations between matter and energy in the universe can therefore be understood in terms of resonance – the transmission and absorption of information and/or energy between resonating objects.

We believe that information in the universe also moves, is transmitted and absorbed through a sort of resonance. We refer to the means or medium through which information moves, is shared, and can be found as subtle reality or the connected mind. This medium has also been called the collective unconscious, spirit world, 4th dimension, Akasha, original medium, holomovement, or implicate order, among other names, and it was referred to simply as the *aether* by scientists until the early 19th century; a medium that was thought to infuse and permeate all space. Some scientists, notably luminary Nikola Tesla, whose genius is only now being recognized and appreciated, never let go of the idea that an information-carrying aether permeated all matter, space and time throughout the universe.

The idea of aether may seem outdated, as it has been discredited as having anything to do with light and gravity. However, the transmission of information through the universe is not yet well understood scientifically, and the whole idea that information permeates the universe like energy or gravity has largely been ignored by the scientific community until recently. This trend has shifted, however, as information theory has emerged as the new central discipline,[29] central since it encompasses mathematics, statistics, economics, communication theory, computer science, genetics and physics.

Theoretical physicist John Archibald Wheeler is acknowledged to have started this profound shift in the scientific community in the early 1990s, having suggested that scientists "regard the physical world as made of information, with energy and matter as incidentals."[30] Most physicists would, I'm sure, cringe at our suggestion that subtle reality informs, shapes and creates physical reality, but to us it seems that we are saying exactly the same thing. Only we propose that information in the universe can be directly accessed, understood and even shaped and manipulated through the connected mind, whereas the disciplines of physics and information theory seek to understand the flow of information through the universe through mathematics and observation.

Resonance in subtle reality doesn't follow logical material rules and entire books could and have been dedicated to the subject. We all intuitively understand resonance though. Certain things and energies just go together: motorcycles and leather, football and beer, peas and carrots, feather boas and Broadway entertainers, children and cartoons, nerds and sci-fi, hippies and peace, psychics and crystals, etc. Resonance is associative, as well as polar; in other words, like attracts like, but opposites – yin and yang energies – can also resonate and complement one another, much like harmonic as well as anharmonic sounds can both be musically pleasing.

Your dreams can give you some insight into the very strange and illogical dynamics of resonance in subtle reality: dreams often follow resonant pathways; for example, you might dream of a blue butterfly landing on your hand, then suddenly it's Tuesday, you're in kindergarten and running for the ice cream truck. Somehow, in your mind and your dreams, like in your early pre-language years, blue butterflies, Tuesdays, and ice cream trucks go together, or resonate with one another. We often understand these strange resonances perfectly in our dreams, and how there can be some essential essence at the core of very different things that makes them fit together, but when we wake up and we get back into our survivor mind we can't make sense of the strange understandings we had in our dream or the morphing pathways we remember our dreams having followed.

The most notable scientific work compiled to date on the

transmission of information through resonance is by biologist Rupert Sheldrake. In his numerous books including *The Presence of the Past, Dogs That Know When Their Owners Are Coming Home* and *Morphic Resonance,* Sheldrake explains that all of nature, from molecules to animals, to entire ecosystems, has a collective memory that functions through a sort of telepathic connection. Collective memories are shared, or expressed, in particular between beings, objects and substances that share the same morphology, or physical form.

Much like well-tuned guitars in a guitar store, all physical forms from atoms, to molecules, to bacteria, to animals, to people, to planets, to galaxies that share the same form will tend to resonate with, absorb and express the same collective memories, and function or behave in similar ways as a result. In general, this means that the laws of nature are more like habits, or collective agreements as to how physical reality should function. In fact, rather than immutable laws, Sheldrake explains that the laws of physics are more like fluctuating ideas that are precisely tuned to harmonize with one another and to permit the existence of the universe we live in and intelligent life.

In biology, the collective memory of nature means that life learns, remembers and shares its knowledge across members of a species or groups of resonant organisms. Animal behaviors we have labeled instinct or biological drives are the result of this collective memory, and not purely the result of genetics. DNA and genes serve as antennas of sorts for resonant collective memories, and are the blueprints for proteins, the building blocks of life through which the collective memories of nature construct themselves into physical forms. Sheldrake has consolidated a great number of studies in biology that have documented how learned behaviors are transmitted from generation to generation, and even across continents, between unrelated members of a number of animal species, without direct physical communication or contact. Learned behaviors that various biologists have documented spreading at speeds and across distances that can only be explained through a sort of telepathy range from the speed at which rats learn to navigate mazes, to birds learning to steal cream from milk bottles, to monkeys washing food, to cockroaches learning not to eat glucose because it was once commonly used as bait to carry insecticides (until cockroaches spontaneously and collectively learned not to eat it).

For humans, morphic resonance shows up in the previously mentioned studies of social networks and the spread of trends, but also in phenomena such as transgenerational trauma transmission. Transgenerational trauma is a very well documented phenomenon where the children and successive generations of the victims of trauma display symptoms of posttraumatic stress related to their parents' or ancestors' initial trauma. On the positive side, in a world where we share our memories and our minds, morphic resonance means that once someone has learned or accomplished something, other people can do so more easily. We can see this effect across many sports, where records are broken year after year, and particularly in extreme sports, simply by scrolling through YouTube videos.

The rapid progression of skills and abilities of skateboarders, BMXers and even hula hoopers through time is readily apparent to anyone viewing YouTube clips in which eleven and twelve year olds now are regularly and widely filming themselves doing tricks that, a few years ago, only a few top professionals could perform. More mundane pursuits are by no means exempt though as one study of morphic resonance showed that people who complete newspaper crosswords the day after they are published solve them more easily, and with higher success rates, than people who attempt the crosswords on the day of publication.

What I think is most important about the realization that we are all telepathically influenced by collective memories is the accompanying realization that, as conscious beings, we can choose which collective memories, and subtle realities, to tune into, focus on, and therefore express in our lives and bodies. If cancer or obesity runs in your family, you are more likely to be obese, or get cancer, but you are not destined to. You have the ability to tune out of and detach yourself from the subtle realities or collective memories that express themselves as obesity and cancer, and tune into and express subtle realities in your body and life related to health and well-being.

Morphic resonance – the idea that information structures, or collective memories, express themselves through resonant forms – partly tells us how we can tune out of unwanted subtle realities and tune into desired subtle realities: we can form our lives and our bodies to resonate with the ideas and collective memories we wish to express. On a basic level, this means that all of our lifestyle choices, the forms of our lives, from the food we eat, to the homes we live in, to the clothes we wear, to the activities we engage in effect the collective memories, subtle realities, or ideas about who we are that we are tuned into. Everything we do, say, think, feel and focus on has meaning, and far-reaching effects. If we want to tune into and express different ideas about who we are, we can do so by changing our thinking, our focus, and the form of our lives, by choosing thoughts, entertainment, nutrition, clothes, environments, friends, activities, work and ways of being that resonate with the ideas, subtle realities or collective memories we want to experience, be influenced by and express in our lives.

In simple terms, fake it until you make it. Synchronicities and spontaneous knowings of all sorts will show up to help you make it. A great example of how this can work comes from actor Nicolas Cage, who told a story about his preparation for his role in *Leaving Las Vegas* while promoting the film. Nick explained that, while preparing for his role as John O'Brien, who the lead character is based on, to become Mr. O'Brien, he bought several suits, and a watch from a pawnshop, that he thought Mr. O'Brien might have worn. When he showed up in character to meet Mr. O'Brien's family, they informed him that he had unknowingly purchased and was wearing the very same model of Rolex that Mr. O'Brien had actually worn in life. A coincidence perhaps, or a great example of how tuning into someone, or something, pulls related information, ideas and subtle realities into your awareness that will play out in your life, if you let them.

On a more conscious level, when we become aware that our minds are awash with telepathic information all the time, we can learn to discern the qualities and sources of our thoughts, and choose which thoughts to focus on and express in our lives, and which ones to ignore. We become conscious in subtle reality when we realize that many of our thoughts, being collective memories that unconsciously drive our behavior if we allow them to, are not our thoughts in the first place: they are collective memories, ideas about who we are, or subtle realities that we can tune into or out of at will through focus. We can let these ideas unconsciously play us, or we can consciously play them like keys on a piano in ways that fulfill, enliven, empower and serve us and everyone else on the planet. We can be who we want to be, firmly grounded in a deep understanding of who we are, while simultaneously being free to playfully become who we want to be in any moment. Life becomes richer, and much more interesting, not just because we are free and empowered, but because every moment is informed through our subtle senses, as well as our physical senses, and we become consciously aware of parts of ourselves we didn't know existed, and a whole new universe.

Tours of (Personal) Subtle Reality

Reality, as you currently experience it, is something like a waking dream. It is disguising deeper and more intensified levels of being and knowing. For those who are ready and willing, the doors to those other levels now stand open.
~ Daniel Pinchbeck

A psychic reading can be thought of as a tour of a sitter's personal subtle realities, where the psychic takes on the role of tour guide and provides a verbal commentary of what they perceive as they tour through the subtle realities a sitter is connected to, for the sitter's benefit. Such tours can be haphazard and aimless, more for entertainment than of specific use, or they may be undertaken with specific intentions, for useful purposes and ends. Unfortunately, many people are so busy focusing on whether psychics are for real or any good, and are so awed when a psychic gets one or two facts right, that they don't notice how useful psychic information can be, or spend any time and effort working *with* a psychic toward purposeful ends.

This focus on entertainment and awe is, I think, a cultural artifact from the late 1800s, when carnivals, sideshows and the spiritualist movement were showcased for entertainment along with oddities and magic shows. Psychic abilities unfortunately became culturally intertwined with entertainment, trickery and showmanship in the midst of a puritanical culture. Hopefully, we can let go of this focus on entertainment and awe. We can still notice that connected mind abilities are amazing. I'm still awed by them myself all the time, but if we can't get past entertainment and awe at the fact that these abilities are real, we will never get to explore what can be done with these abilities. Connected mind adepts cannot get us there alone though, no matter how skilled or amazing their abilities are. The quality and effectiveness of our work depends on the knowledge, focus, attitude and skill of our sitters, as much or more than it depends on our abilities.

The important thing to understand about any telepathic work is that it is a team effort, the quality of which will depend on the combined efforts and abilities of the telepath, subjects, observers and sitters. Some psychics may be able to get some information and even impressive validations without the cooperation of sitters, with skeptical observers looking on. It's tougher to do, takes far more energy and is nowhere near as productive as working with cooperative sitters and observers though. To give you an example of how easily a session can be derailed, even with cooperative sitters who understand the process, I'll share a few details of a recent session where I sat down with university professor Imants Baruss, who asked me to contact physicist Richard Feynman.

Although Feynman was one of the best-known scientists in the world in the 70s and 80s, and is considered to be one of the greatest physicists of all time, I didn't know who he was at the time, or even that he was a physicist. I've never taken a physics course in my life and sadly only have grade 9 science. I provided a number of pieces of identifying information, including that Richard had passed from something kidney related, which Imants did not believe was correct. To validate Richard's identity, Imants asked if Richard could provide the value of the fine structure constant, again something which I knew nothing about, but Richard would apparently have known. Richard started to give me the number "0.085…", however, Imants indicated that this was not correct. He was looking for the number 137, which is apparently the accepted and well-known value for the fine structure constant. I insisted that there were more digits but Imants moved on. The session seemed like a failure, until, Imants tells me, he was talking about the session on the phone with his collaborating colleague, and their phone connection cut out, at which point his colleague noticed the number "0.08" on her desk calculator.

Further subsequent research revealed the following quote from Feynman's 1985 book, *QED: The Strange Theory of Light and Matter*: "There is a most profound and beautiful question associated with the observed coupling constant, e – the amplitude for a real electron to emit or absorb a real photon. It is a simple number that has been experimentally determined to be close to 0.08542455. (My physicist friends won't recognize this number, because they like to remember it as the inverse of its square: about 137.03597 with about an uncertainty of about 2 in the last decimal place. It has been a mystery ever since it was discovered more than fifty years ago, and all good theoretical physicists put this number up on their wall and worry about it.)" Later, after watching a documentary on Richard's life, I didn't even feel the need to let Imants know that the documentary told the story of how Richard had died of cancer, which initially originated in his kidney.

Insisting that sessions go a particular way, or expecting specific information to come through, without considering the information that is coming through can quickly derail any telepathic work. Everyone involved needs to be open and willing to go with the flow of information, and most importantly of all, the sitter, or subject of the session. As a sitter, letting a telepath or psychic in to take an unhindered tour of your subtle realities, and connect, connected mind to connected mind, you need to open up, which can feel very vulnerable. Ideally, when a sitter has some connected mind ability, sitter and telepath tour a sitter's subtle realities together: simultaneous, combined focus makes a sitter's subtle realities easier to perceive and more potent. As a sitter or observer, you can follow such tours in your own connected mind, experiencing a session rather than just listening to and thinking about the conversation. You don't need as many words to understand what the telepath is talking about as she describes subtle realities. As a sitter, you will walk away with a deeper experience and understanding of your own subtle realities, far more conscious of your drivers and issues than you would have been had you only followed the tour of your subtle realities with your analytical survivor mind.

You don't have to be skilled with your connected mind to benefit from a telepathic tour of your subtle realities though, nor do you have to follow along with your own connected mind. Simply opening up through verbal conversation has the effect of opening yourself to the telepathic tour. In other words, be present and available to participate in the moment. Withholding information, not opening up through verbal conversation, or bringing a mistrusting energy to a session has the effect of blocking the telepathic connection and the tour. It makes a telepath's work as a tour guide much more difficult, and it's not just that a closed off sitter's subtle realities are more difficult to perceive: without a sitter's feedback to give context and meaning to the subtle realities a telepath is seeing, it's much more difficult for a telepath to know exactly what he or she is looking at, why, and where to look next. Without a sitter's cooperation, sessions can be more like a series of random statements than a coherent, purposeful journey.

To people who do not understand the need for a sitter's cooperation in the telepathic tour process, whose focus is on testing a psychic, or on the entertainment and awe aspect of a psychic reading, withholding information seems like a logical part of the show and a good way to test a psychic. I get it. The desire to test a psychic is understandable. The way it's typically done though tends to backfire, and creates the result that it is intended to avoid. The more distrust a sitter has for their psychic, or the process, the more they close themselves off from the telepathic tour, and the quality of the reading will reflect this. It's a catch-22 if you're trying to find a good psychic and don't know anyone who can recommend or refer you to a great one, as well as for skeptics and investigators who don't understand the process and aren't willing to trust enough to actually participate in the process and make a fair assessment.

Testing a telepath by not opening up or withholding information can also warp the telepath's perception of your subtle realities by limiting the subtle realities they have access to. Without the cooperation of a sitter, a telepath is left to pick up on what subtle realities he or she can, which, I suspect, will likely be only the most potent ones. These potent subtle realities may be the most logical ones to guess, giving skeptics fodder to dismiss psychic information as logical guessing. In the worst-case scenario, where a psychic has limited abilities and is focused on the awe factor, some of the easiest subtle realities to perceive will be subtle realities that are potent because they are emotionally charged. Amateur psychics could, I suppose, prey upon people's past traumas and fears to look more powerful and important, but I like to think that people just don't know any better, not that they are inherently bad people. The ominous warnings and dire predictions that might result from such interactions only serve to enhance the potency of the feared subtle realities and past traumas, making them more likely to come true or repeat.

Just as there are bad and even predatory lawyers, doctors and priests in the world, I'm sure that there are also bad and predatory psychics. Just because someone has enough psychic ability, what I term receptivity, to pick up on a few relevant subtle realities does not mean they are a good telepath, or someone you should listen to. There are many receptive people in the world for which receptivity is a great detriment because it is uncontrolled or because it makes life overwhelming and confusing. Many of these people can be found on street corners, or in mental health institutions, unable to control or integrate their telepathic experiences of the world with daily living. Although being receptive does make you psychic, receptivity is just one of many connected skills and abilities necessary to competently navigate and use the connected mind. The job of any psychic, at a minimum, should be to guide you safely towards self-insight, joy and fulfilment in your life, not to scare you by reiterating all your fears and focusing on all the bad things that might happen to you.

So, telepathy and psychic readings are made possible partly because once a thought has its own independent existence in the connected mind (as a subtle reality) anyone who is consciously able to navigate the connected mind can perceive it. This does not mean that your entire mind is open for anyone to tour. Although subtle realities may be perceived by anyone in the connected mind, finding specific subtle realities, understanding what you are looking at, how they are connected to the real world, or to whom a subtle reality is connected is another feat altogether. The connected mind is a very, very big place. Words like infinite are used to describe it in many religions and traditions for a reason. So, although your thoughts and the subtle realities that you identify with as You may not be uniquely your own, you are still unique. Who you are, what makes you You, can be thought of as the unique connections and combinations you have to many subtle realities, some of which are relatively individual, and others that are shared to varying degrees, with family, friends, your community and the wider world.

The strange implication of the independent existence of subtle realities is that anyone who perceives a subtle reality can also shape it, add to it and connect with it so that it becomes part of their own subtle reality. When developing or working towards a vision or goal, whether it's a new year resolution, a business plan or vision for your life, be careful who you share your ideas with. The subtle realities you are forming and shaping through the visioning process will become more potent as more people connect to them, but judgmental or jealous naysayers and doubters can do more than just sap your confidence. Ownership of subtle realities is meaningless, what matters is who is connected to a subtle reality, and how each connection synergetically shapes that subtle reality.

The subtle realities you are connected to are not uniquely your own, but are continually shaped by everyone who is connected to them, and by each person who connects to, or severs, their connection with that subtle reality. From this perspective, who you are and who you become is shaped by, and is a reflection of, everyone and everything connected to you through subtle reality. Your family, friends, enemies, coworkers, acquaintances, your home, the objects in your home, your pets, the wider community you share your mind with and, really, everyone and everything on the planet shapes and influences who you are. There is no escaping the fact that we are all deeply and profoundly interconnected, and that what effects any one of us, any living being, or network of living beings on the planet, great or small, affects us all.

Getting to know someone (or something), really understanding who someone (or something) is on a very deep level, is best accomplished by taking an extended tour through that person's (or thing's) subtle realities. This is something we all do, all the time, though mostly unconsciously, without noticing the nonverbal conversations that always occur alongside our verbal conversations in life. Tours of subtle reality are the most basic form of relationship, connection, and telepathic communication. These tours are facilitated through explicit verbal conversations between living people, and occur when both parties are present in the spiritual sense of the word. Presence, and awareness of the nonverbal, as well as the verbal conversation, is often referred to as *active listening* or *listening with your third ear* in business circles. Ideally, both parties are consciously aware of the nonverbal conversation as well as the verbal conversation, but let's not hold our breath just yet since most people entirely dismiss and deny their telepathic experience.

The more consciously aware of the nonverbal conversation

participants are, the less important the words become, the richer and more vibrant the inner experience of everyone involved is, and the clearer and deeper the meaning and understanding resulting from the conversation will be. When the survivor mind is absent from such conversations, communication is very much mind to mind. Subtle realities and meanings are swapped back and forth directly from connected mind to connected mind, without the logic, filters, projections, manipulations and fears of the survivor mind getting in the way. These are the types of conversations that we refer to as meaningful; where we are left with a sense of peace, completion, wholeness, understanding and perhaps even awe afterwards. We walk away feeling like we just experienced a real connection or had a sacred experience. I am convinced that the greatest gift you can give others is your presence and full attention without the desire to help, fix, change, pity, analyze or judge.

We know that people crave being heard, being understood and being seen for who they are. We also know that you can have someone hear your words without listening to you, or truly seeing who you are. What we are really crave as a basic human need, I think, is telepathic connection – the connection we experience when we give our full attention and presence to someone, or receive someone's full attention and presence. We *all* need telepathic connection and we are not broken, needy, or defective for needing this attention.

Telepathic connections feed, nourish and energize us in deep and profound ways. Dead people show me that they light up and become *more alive* when we focus on them, or telepathically connect with them. Living people and animals certainly *light up* and come to life when we give them our undivided, loving attention. Babies only grow and thrive when they receive regular doses of love, affection and attention, showing us just how much we need love and connection. Babies whose physical needs are taken care of, but who are not touched, loved and paid attention to, wither and die, as overwhelmed orphanages around the world have painfully learned in the past. By giving children our love and attention, we are actually energetically feeding and nourishing them, while solidifying and enhancing who they are by making their subtle realities more potent. When we can be present and pay attention, we actually support them in living into who they are. You can call it love but it's more than the conventional concept of what love is.

Your loving presence and attention to another person – little or big – may actually be the key to the growth, health, and well-being of others. In sitting with a conscious and present telepath, opening up and sharing your subtle realities in their loving presence, or connecting with anyone with a deeply loving presence, you are nourishing yourself through connection, and enhancing and solidifying who you are in the process. In giving your full attention to others, your loving presence, without the desire to help, fix, change, pity, analyze or judge, you are also nourishing and lighting up anyone you chose to give this gift to into a brighter, healthier, more alive person. It is one of the greatest gifts you can share with the world. One I hope you will share.

Win-Win-Win Changes Everything

But if all maximizing models are really arguing is that "people will always seek to maximize something," then they obviously can't predict anything, which means employing them can hardly be said to make anthropology more scientific. All they really add to analysis is a set of assumptions about human nature. The assumption, most of all, that no one ever does anything primarily out of concern for others; that whatever one does, one is only trying to get something out of it for oneself. In common English, there is a word for this attitude. It's called "cynicism." Most of us try to avoid people who take it too much to heart. In economics, apparently, they call it "science."

~ David Graeber, *Toward an Anthropological Theory of Value: The False Coin of Our Own Dreams*

When I was a teenager I lived in New York City for a while, in the Gramercy Park Hotel on the corner of 21st and Lexington Avenue. On the Friday of the July long weekend, I was getting off the subway returning home from my last appointment. As I surfaced to street level, I was counting my money. The upside was it was easy to count, since I only had a dollar in change. The downside, the handful of change was the sum total of all of my money. With payday on Monday, and Monday a holiday, I realized that I only had a dollar to live on for the next three days. As I walked down Park Avenue staring into the bleak pile of change in my hand, I quickly realized, but somehow accepted, the fullness of my fate. I was screwed, and probably not going to eat for three days, which, as a model in the 80s, did have an upside. At that moment a homeless person, spotting the change in my hand, put out their hand. I stopped, looked into my palm, and decided to split my money in half, giving the homeless man fifty cents and saving fifty cents for a Diet Coke to treat myself in preparation for was about to be a truly long weekend. Yes, Diet Coke was only fifty cents back then.

I passed my hotel and walked to the corner store where I went straight to the fridge and grabbed a Diet Coke. As I stood at the counter to pay, I noticed two crisp one hundred dollar bills lying in the muffin tray to the left of the checkout. I looked around, but there was no one in the store. I held up the money and asked the guy at the checkout about it. He had no idea. The store had been empty for a long time. Since it was just me and the cashier in the store, I offered to split the two hundred bucks with him. I left the store with a Diet Coke and a hundred dollars.

As I walked to the front desk at the Gramercy Park Hotel to collect my mail, the front desk clerk Shiel asked if I would like to take his free dinner passes for the night to a new restaurant down the street. He wasn't off work until eleven, so a sit-down dinner was out of the question. The dinner was five courses and included a complimentary bottle of wine. The dinner was for two, so I took my roommate Rachel, who was also broke, but kindly left the tip. I was full and I still had a hundred dollars to get me through the weekend. Rachel and I returned to the hotel just as Shiel was finishing work. I'm sure we were festive from the wine at dinner and a belly full of delicious free food. Shiel asked us if we'd like to go out to a club, on him. My night of drinks and dancing in a New York club concluded when I found a bag of weed in the middle of a crosswalk, on the way back to the hotel. For some of you this would have been scary, but to me it was the icing on the cake of my day!

I've revisited this experience in my mind hundreds of times over the years, trying to understand how it all came to be. I now think that splitting my four quarters with the homeless guy was kind of like making a slit in an intricately folded piece of paper. When the paper gets unfolded, that one slit shows up in multiple places, like in a paper snowflake. But that's only the case when you're in connection, connected to the place where all the paper is folded up together and touching, what I now understand as subtle reality. On that July weekend, I had accepted my fate. I didn't fear my broke starving weekend, I embraced it, stayed in connection, and watched a beautiful snowflake unfold. Moments later, the fifty cents I gave away became two hundred dollars. By giving away half of that, when I gave the hundred dollar bill to the cashier, I acted without thinking by allowing the greater plan to think for me, from a place of inspiration – I stayed in the flow of what was happening. I gave the cashier the money because there were two bills and there were two of us. It was that simple. It was win-win-win; as if we all knew there was a bigger plan that we were in on. It felt magical, and easy, as life always does when you're in connection.

That additional slit in the folded paper, sharing the hundred dollar bill, kept the pattern in the snowflake going, and expanded it: I gave away my quarters because I could see they weren't going to change anything for me, but they just might for someone else. When I found the two hundred dollars, I knew my needs were going to be met. Splitting it still allowed for that. It just plain felt right. Walking out of the store with money, I could let go even more, knowing all of my basics would get taken care of for the weekend. That acceptance of splitting the last of my money and taking care of someone else spun out and came back to me in the form of food, wine, dancing, drinks and weed; an abundance of all my basic wants and needs as a teenager.

When we take the resistance of the survivor mind out of the equation, life takes on a brilliant ease and flow, and happens at a much faster pace. Our wants and needs are fulfilled in speedy, ingenious and unexpected ways. Life becomes magical. Sometimes very little has to happen to create big results. To create results through connection, however, everyone needs to participate. Everybody needs to be tuned into the larger, collective plan, contribute to its creation, and be willing to let their connected minds and the bigger plan guide and inspire their choices and actions. Had any one player in the coolest day of my life not been willing to go with the flow, play in the moment, and do what felt right, I would have ended up hungry and broke while everyone around me celebrated the long weekend.

I've had many similarly magical experiences in life since that day, and have learned, to some extent, how to intentionally create them. I can tell you that intention, connection and keen discernment without resistance are paramount, along with a willingness to trust the greater plan, even if you don't know where it's leading you. Most important of all, though, is finding other conscious people in connection to co-create with, and avoiding those who are not. No matter how in alignment you are, how connected you are, or how brilliant you are at navigating with your connected mind, try and co-create with the wrong people, in the wrong environment, and the results are bound to be painful and potentially disastrous. Creativity, personal freedom, keen insight into how things are and a willingness to tell it like it is can be deeply threatening to anyone who is deeply entrenched in a survivor-minded society. What I can tell you, though, is that you are not powerless or completely dependent on whether or not everyone else around you is in connection or not.

Like Marianne Williamson says: as you let your own light shine, you unconsciously give others permission to do the same. We all have lights that shine very brightly in subtle reality, if we let them, even if we sometimes have to keep a low profile in physical reality so as not to pose a threat or an easy target to survivor-minded people who can only judge, denigrate, threaten and fearfully insist that everyone repeat worn-out patterns of living and being. We are all capable of cutting the fabric of reality where it's all folded together in the perfect spot to telepathically orchestrate desired events in our lives and create beautiful snowflakes, no matter what our circumstances. The more you live your own life in your connected mind, the more joy filled, loving and playful you are willing to be, the more you invite everyone else in your life to do the same. You can't explain connection in words to most people, and you most certainly can't argue or convince others into connection, but you can inspire others through your own being. Not everyone will join you, but a good contact high is hard to pass up. It might not always work, but it is surprising how often and quickly connection can make or save your day.

I recently crossed an international border with a car full of people. To my horror, the border guard informed me that my passport had expired, almost a year prior. It hadn't occurred to me to check the expiry date before I left. There was no way I should have been allowed across the border, especially because it turned out our car was full of contraband… tangerines, grapes and a number of other fruits that are forbidden from crossing international borders (other than by plane with other fruit apparently). We failed just about every question we were asked, and yet… to the astonishment of everyone in the car, somewhere in the laughter and connection that ensued from each successive violation of international law, the delightful man under the stern demeanor and a uniform with a gun decided to let us pass. My dear friend in the back seat, laughing hysterically with relief as we drove across the border, summed up the interaction simply by saying, "These aren't the droids you're looking for."

Working as a telepath for fifteen years or so, I have watched and experienced the significant and formative events of a few thousand people's lives in my mind. I'd like to tell you that my work and daily experience of the world as a telepath is always inspiring, heartwarming and gratifying. It's not. It can be heartbreaking. Out of fairness, I do have to advise anyone wanting to become more conscious and more telepathic themselves that the world we live in, as well as the lives and minds of most of the people who live in it, are not always pleasant to perceive telepathically. The ideas and philosophies we've chosen to build modern society upon are deeply out of alignment with our cooperative, connected, telepathic (spiritual if you wish) nature. Very simply, much of our culture, especially the world of media, business, commerce and law is survivor mind based. The ways in which society insists most of the exchanges and interactions of our lives must happen are not conducive to the co-creative, synergistic orchestrations of the connected mind. Most people's lives are heartbreakingly limited by the little boxes and lists of survivor mind rules they are forced to or force themselves to live by. In a survivor mind-based society, with barriers, controls and costs at every turn, we are largely crabs in a bucket, pulling one another down and keeping one another trapped. I do see this changing, though, and hope the pace accelerates.

As more and more people wake up and embrace the power of life in connection and cooperation, the more powerful telepathy as a technology becomes. The speed and ease with which conscious, connected individuals, groups and organizations can co-create win-win-win solutions for their benefit and the benefit of everyone on the planet will also increase. Companies, cooperatives, organizations and communities that embrace the power and genius of inspired and connected people working together in collective synergy towards win-win-win solutions will create ingenious, amazing results and rewards that will benefit everyone involved, and the planet. Companies and organizations that are out of alignment with excellence and the greater good will simply not be able to compete.

Telepathic consumers, communities and populations will no longer be fooled by marketers and profit-driven organizations that promote and peddle products that don't live up to their marketing hype and come at the expense of the other people, beings, or the ecosystems we live in and cherish. The care, love, passion and quality that goes into the production of any good, from food to furniture, can be felt by anyone with telepathic ability. The presence of toxic chemicals, along with any traumas associated with the production of any good, especially food, is easily discerned by conscious, telepathic individuals. The food choices of awakening consumers around the world who are now insisting on quality, organic, sustainably and ethically grown foods, and can taste the difference, reflect the emergence of this trend.

Similarly, the sincerity, genuineness and ability of political candidates to make good on promises can be discerned by conscious, telepathic voters. Sociopathic politicians who promise renewal and change but uphold the status quo and make backroom deals to line the pockets of corporations gunning for profits at any cost will no longer be able to sway telepathic populations with clever words. *Connected mind technology, collectively learning to navigate our own consciousness, and collectively using our natural telepathy may be what is needed to save our planet and co-create a wondrous, safe and abundant future. Everything changes when we collectively wake up. Many of us are already awake though, so the real question is: "What do we do now?"*

Really, win-win-win, or collective synergy, is the only way forward. In a telepathic, holographic world, you only win when everyone else wins. You are not isolated from the misery, suffering or ill health of anyone else on the planet, your environment, other beings on the planet, or our planet herself. Your happiness, well-being and abundance is a direct reflection of the happiness, well-being and abundance of everyone and everything around you, far and wide. The only way to watch out for number one, to take care of oneself, is to take care of the earth and every person and being on it. Our success in this endeavor will partly depend on science and technology, along with our collective recognition that our survivor minds have lead us astray. Mostly though, I think, our success will depend on our collective ability to embrace and use the part of ourselves that is ingeniously equipped to synergistically orchestrate the fulfilment of everyone's wants and needs: the connected mind.

So what can *you* do now? How can you find connection and balance today, and be the change you want to see in the world? How can you make your own tiny slits in the folded paper where everything is connected, slits that will magnify and propagate through the snowflake of the world in powerful and far-reaching ways? In closing, I leave you with a few of the most common ideas I am inspired to share, ideas that will orient you in the world in a very particular way to offer connection at every turn, and inspire others to do the same:

- Remember, connection is free and available for you to choose any time, all the time; whether you choose to participate or not is up to you.

- Intend and align with your greatest good, the greatest good of the people you're with and the greatest good for all, in all that you do.

- Trust the astounding wisdom and intelligence that is a part of you. Let your connected mind guide and inspire you to magical experiences and solutions. Accept what is happening in the moment to allow your connected mind to flow you into the next moment with ease and grace. Follow your inspiration and bliss and dare to say yes, even when the path is so thrilling it's scary.

- Dare to say no. Fiercely guard your energy, happiness and well-being against draining dramas, arguments and fights where there can be no winners. Stay in your integrity. If something doesn't feel right and you're in connection, a wise and intelligent part of yourself is giving you actual information about the outcome of the path you are about to embark upon. Save yourself and others stress, heartache and pain by having the courage and conviction to make a different choice, or create a different path. You always have choices.

- Invite others who are receptive into connection through your own radiance and loving presence. Have the wisdom to let those who find your radiance and joy irritating, threatening or painful be as they are while still patiently seeking to identify rather than judge or compare. Look first to see the essential goodness in people. It's there, in everyone. Go for connection first, especially if you want something badly enough to fight for it; you're more likely to get what you want or better by finding a win for all oriented solution through connection.

More simply and importantly…

- Take time to be silent and still, in stillness and receptivity you will find connection, inspiration and wisdom.

- Fall in love with something and go and do that. In leisure, in life, in your home, and in your career. Everyone needs a thing, or two, or three… Lose yourself in something you love as often as you can (you'll always come back, I promise).

- Move, breathe, participate and engage in whatever ways you are inspired. Movement brings you into connection. Take some time to wonder and perceive during your run, bike ride, while dancing, or in yoga class, and especially in the stillness that follows. You've worked hard to alter your state, you might as well make use of it.

- Eat for connection. Get back into alignment with your own

body by eating foods that are full of life force, grown and prepared with love and attention. Being sick, slow, overweight, dissociated and miserable is not our natural state and isn't conducive to connection.

- Stay curious and follow your curiosity. Pay attention to your body, thoughts and feelings, especially unusual sensations, images and knowings. Notice. Let your curiosity reveal the many connections between your inner experiences and your outer world (but don't feel the need to overshare, your inner experiences and revelations about the nature of the universe may be frightening to some).

and most importantly…

- Love. Love fiercely and playfully with an open hand. Love with all your being, without expectation or condition in all that you do. Love is a powerful ability, the key to telepathic connection and the driving force of conscious co-creation for the greatest good of all.

Welcome back to your natural state.

Epilogue – Telepathic Conversations

To be, or not to be: that is the question:
Whether 'tis nobler in the mind to suffer the slings and arrows of outrageous fortune,
Or to take arms against a sea of troubles, and by opposing end them?

To die: to sleep no more;
and by a sleep to say we end the heart-ache
and the thousand natural shocks that flesh is heir to,
'tis a consummation devoutly to be wish'd.

To die, to sleep; to sleep: perchance to dream: ay, there's the rub;
For in that sleep of death what dreams may come
when we have shuffled off this mortal coil.
~ Hamlet in Shakespeare's *Hamlet*

I really don't consider myself a stage medium, nor do I consider gallery readings my strong suit, or something I really enjoy. I do still seem to end up in front of large groups of people, facilitating conversations with their dead people a lot though. I've learned a lot about telepathic communication through the process, particularly from some of the stranger things that have happened. One of the mysterious things that consistently happens with many psychic-mediums during group sessions, and I am no exception, is that two or more dead people often ride in on the same information. For example, I may start a group session sensing a man standing beside me, who shows me his hands to tell me that he works with his hands for a living. I might get a sense of his build and age, or not. Age and build are tricky identifying factors because, of course, they change over the course of people's lifetimes. I get most of my information visually, so I might see the letters "Feb" flash through my awareness. This man might put his hand on his heart. I'll say something like, "I've got a man here with a February birthday or passing. He works with his hands and tells me he passes from a heart attack."

Although I've said there are no words in the connected mind, it's not entirely unheard of for a dead person to write a word or show me a number in my head. The communication is still visual, as I see such words as if they're written on a chalkboard. When it comes to months, I think they come up so often that I've developed a sort of automatic translation response where my mind automatically translates sensory information or clairi-science conveying a month into something I readily understand. I've often said that I feel like my memories are a rolodex for dead people to use since I often have the sensation that dead people are using my memories to convey information to me, although it may be more the case that my mind simply projects the closest resonant image it understands onto blocks of sensory information a dead person has shared. I once had a dead scientist show me that, to communicate telepathically, he "plucks" or "pokes" particular spots in living people's brains, to evoke a sensation or recollection.

One might think that zodiac signs, being visually distinct and well-known, would be a better way to convey months of the year through sensory information. I was never familiar enough with all of the signs of the zodiac for the symbols to work for me and would have been very resistant to my sessions blending into astrology. I don't think there are any hard and fast rules when it comes to communicating telepathically or subtle sensory vocabulary. For the most part, I think you go with what works for you, do your best to learn on the fly, and adapt to the dead people, animals or beings you're communicating with.

Most dead people initially start communicating by identifying themselves and others with a month of birth or death, and sometimes very little in the way of other information; perhaps a cause of death or a gesture to the part of the body that failed. I don't like that the mediumship process often begins with a month of birth or death, especially in large group settings, but months of birth and death seem to be how dead people want the process to unfold, no matter how I feel about it. To a skeptical rational materialist, this first step in the process of gallery mediumship, identifying and sorting out who belongs to who, looks like clear evidence of cold reading: of guessing probable facts and then preying on vulnerable, gullible victims. I think it's the people pointing the finger that are afraid of being vulnerable and fear they are potentially the gullible victims and end up projecting their mistrust onto mediums. Needing to cling to the belief that physical reality is the only reality, they need to believe that the world is full of liars, manipulators and cheats on the one hand, and delusional, gullible victims on the other. But if you only focus on the identifying and sorting process, you're missing the actual show.

Sometimes, four or five people will stand up in response to a man coming through who worked with his hands and, say, passes from a heart attack, all having grandfathers, fathers, uncles or friends who fit the description. Other times no one will stand up, even when I provide much more specific details. It takes a lot of courage to get up in front of an audience, admit that you want to talk to a dead person, and potentially have a very personal and emotional conversation in front of a room full of strangers. More often than not, when I am left hanging and not able to match a dead person coming through with a living audience member in the moment, someone will come to me after the event to tell me that the details I provided matched their dead person exactly. Sometimes, the facts of a dead person's passing, or the personal nature of a situation, are way too sensitive to air in public and I'm happy to provide a few more details or a personal message, but I rarely do readings after a group session. I don't really think it's very fair to leave a medium hanging in front of a large group and then expect a private session after. The people who come to me after gallery sessions, however, just tend to want to let me know that the information I shared was for them, and that it was enough for them to know their dead person was there and said "Hi".

The next thing I might see after a man who passes from a heart attack, who works with his hands, is the number 9, and then another birthday or passing month, say the letters "Apr" in my mind. Information like the number nine sometimes comes with clairiscience, and I just know what the information means, implies or refers to. During the identifying and sorting process, however, this information on its own is rather meaningless. I do know that dead people typically follow a certain protocol in this process and I also have a sort of mental list of questions to intentionally wonder about on my own so that information comes in a particular order and I have an idea about what such information may mean when it comes into my awareness. So, before getting the number 9 and Apr, I might have curiously wondered about something like family, so I know what pops into my mind is about family. Since I know the information is relevant to family, and I can feel the relationships associated, I might say something like: "This person is one of nine. This person also wants me to acknowledge someone with a birthday or passing in April."

Sometimes all but one person sits down, and the one person left standing will say something like, "My father was a carpenter, he died of a heart attack in February, he was one of nine children and my mother's birthday is in April." Now all that may seem like reaching, like someone is trying to make random information match the details of their dead relative's life, but it's the conversations that happen after I know who a dead person belongs to that are interesting. Conversations like: "Your grandmother's homemade cannolis used to have orange rind and chocolate chips in them, and she was known for them, but now you're making them with low fat cheese and no chocolate chips?

She says hers were way better, and she wants me to say to you (in a playful way), 'What kind of self-respecting Italian uses low fat cheese anyway?'" Even without the uncanny conversations that often follow, if you run the rough numbers on even basic identifying facts, the statistics become pretty impressive, and the way dead people seem to like to identify themselves starts to make sense.

If, say, two identifying factors have a one in ten chance of being correct for any given person, like you might roughly estimate a month of death and a cause of death like a heart attack might have, that gives a roughly one in one hundred chance of these two facts fitting a particular person. Each independent coincident identifying factor you add on multiplies the improbability of that set of facts randomly fitting anyone's life. For example, three coincident facts that each independently have a one in ten chance of being correct for any given person give a roughly one in one thousand chance that all three independent facts would randomly fit one particular person, four independent facts would have a one in 10,000 chance of randomly fitting and so on. You can reduce this improbability by making certain facts fit someone's life in multiple ways, or picking and choosing which facts to apply to multiple people; however, multiple coincident facts become very specific identifiers, especially when one or two facts have very low probabilities of fitting anyone's life. For example, the fact that someone was one of nine children has a very low probability of fitting any given person's life, and is a very clear identifying fact.

When you spend any kind of time observing mediumship conversations, the possibility that people are fooling themselves into believing that their dead relatives are talking to them by making random facts fit their lives is so miniscule that no rational person can dismiss mediumship as reaching, cold reading, or being fooled by randomness. Months of death and birth, as well as other basic identifying facts like: male/female, used to color my hair, eye color, used to smoke or drink, sense of humor, loud/quiet, nice versus tactless and honest, great smile, ladies' man, great teeth, great smell, shoe preference and other such fairly generic identifying facts come up all the time. They may be fairly generic, but they are easy to telepathically communicate in visual-sensory terms and, taken together, become very specific. For example, a dead man might telepathically show me just his forearm, a dark blue suit sleeve and crisp white shirt cuff underneath, really nice fabrics, crisp lines, and a great smell. He might also show me "June" and a black Cadillac. I might say something like: "This guy is super cute, he knows how to dress and he smells amazing. When he smiles, his eyes sparkle," which might fit a lot of people, but the black Cadillac and June might make such a description uncannily specific for anyone who knew this man. A woman might show me a pair of red heels, to which her family might respond, "Oh, she wore a lot of red, and loved red heels, we called her the lady in red."

During gallery sessions, seemingly against all odds, a number of people will continue to stand, even when I have explained a number of identifying factors that should make who is talking very clear. Sometimes, people simply share uncannily similar circumstances, for example, two mothers in a group session might both turn out to have lost daughters near their birthdays to suicide. I have to wonder if, in such cases, similarities are deliberately pointed out to bring strangers together who can empathize and support one another. More often than not, what seems to happen in these situations is that a number of dead people are talking to me, all at the same time, some of whom will initially identify themselves together as a group because they resonate from the same series of identifying facts – they have a lot in common.

Sometimes, three out of four facts will fit multiple people, so it's not quite clear which living people a particular batch of information belongs to. In these situations, I think it's more likely that all of the people who stand up are being acknowledged by their dead people; it's just happening all at once, as a group, rather than individually. In some ways, this tactic of saying "hi" to loved ones as a group isn't surprising. I often feel multiple dead people sort of line up waiting to talk before and during group sessions. A couple of them will usually even start talking to me a day before a big group session or in the car on the way to the venue.

Having a number of dead people working together to acknowledge their living people and minimize the time I have to spend to do so makes sense. There is always a lineup of dead people who want to communicate with living audience members whenever I do a group of any size. From the other side, my mind must seem a little bit like the merge lanes where multiple highways come together, or like twenty telephone lines all leading to the same phone. Compressing data so to speak and maximizing the number of people who are acknowledged in this way actually makes sense if you think about it, especially since I don't experience the same sort of problems during individual readings or with small groups where everyone has sufficient time to connect with their own dead people.

As the sorting and focusing process goes, dead people will usually drop out of such conversations one by one, as soon as they get a strong validation and a message or two through to their living person. Sometimes no one drops out of the conversation though; sometimes, I actually have to conduct two or more conversations at the same time. Often, it's simply that people who were pushy and loud in life are the ones who talk first. Some dead people can't stop talking, sometimes interjecting over multiple readings over the course of a session. The important part of group sessions to the dead people who come through, however, doesn't seem to be how I look, that readings go smoothly, or that I get widely understandable validations that prove their existence. The most important part of the exercise for dead people seems to be what happens in their loved ones' hearts and minds. Conversations often wrap the moment I see connection happen in a living person. Like the moment the Grinch's heart grows, I can see the love and connection radiate out from inside of people the moment they truly know their person is present.

Once I can focus in on one dead person and his or her family, I'll get all kinds of other more specific details. In the instance of the man who works with his hands who passes from a heart attack, he might show me the main highway through London, Canada, where I live, and he'll take me one direction, then show me a landmark I recognize. I'll say, "He's from Windsor?" I might get: "Yes", or "That's where I'm living now", or "He was born in Detroit, which is just across the river." I have a pretty clear sign for American, a sort of pulling down feeling that signifies south, or not from here.

I might be shown details about the family and connections, given a tour of the family home, meals and favorite pastimes, saying something like, "Okay, he's showing me a bungalow with white siding, it used to be blue, the kitchen is to the side and shows me his favorite chair in the basement, that's where he spends most of his time. Who's the October birthday? She's special. They hung out there together. Now he's showing me potato salad on the picnic table out back, and red Jell-O but there's something I'm supposed to say about it, or everyone argues about what goes in it. You're playing on a tire swing..." The response to this flood of details that often follows someone identifying or claiming a dead person communicating to me is a string of yeses, and explanations of how each of these details is from these people's shared life together. Tears often flow.

I will also often be shown a scene from the recent life events of the person I'm focusing on, or their family, for example, a new grandchild, a new job or a bizarre incident at a recent family event. Dead people will occasionally reference the ways they have tried to communicate, like showing up in dreams, stopping clocks, getting clocks to chime, opening doors, flickering specific lights or leaving feathers or pennies in odd places. Sometimes I get validations that a loved one is still present in living people's lives in specific ways. "You talk to him all the time, you were just doing it the other day when you were brushing your teeth?" or "You were gardening recently and talking to your mother?" The response to such questions is usually followed by explanations like:

"I never garden, I haven't in years, but I decided to go out and pick some weeds yesterday."

"Yes, and you were talking to her?"

"Yes, she used to love to garden."

"Well she knows all about it. She says you don't have to talk to her out loud though."

"I know, I just prefer to."

Most exchanges are shorter, some as simple as a single validation to say "Hi". Sometimes the hello is not even for the living person I'm talking to, or even for someone present in an audience. For example, in front of a group of about three hundred people, I was once given only the image of Henry Fonda in the movie *On Golden Pond* for a man's daughter, who I'll call Sally, who was in the audience. Sally had raised her hand and asked if her father had a message for her and her mother. Sally insisted that she didn't know what my Henry Fonda reference meant, and that it didn't have anything to do with her father. I wasn't getting any more information so I had to move on. I felt like a total fool. It must have looked like an epic failure to watch. I received an e-mail the next day from Sally, telling me that when she told her mother what had happened, her mother laughed, shook her head, and reminded Sally that everyone always said that her father looked just like Henry Fonda, and couldn't believe that she didn't remember that.

It's amazing how many people go blank in the moment, even when provided with a clear piece of identifying information, as well as how often dead people will use information that doesn't make sense in the moment as their way to say hello to someone who isn't present: a cryptic message that checks out later. For example, I was recently talking to a dead person who referenced Wayne and Garth by showing me the movie *Wayne's World*. This man's living friend had no idea what he was talking about, until months later when he asked his dead friend's mother what these names might mean. Turns out, this man's cats in life were named Wayne and Garth.

What I do consistently notice about the process of mediumship is that I'm often prompted by dead people to say things that make their living people think about or focus on something specific. The direct meaning of what I'm shown or prompted to say isn't always relevant. Sometimes, I even seem to be given incorrect information as a roundabout way to get someone to focus on something specific, which sometimes makes me look like I don't know what I'm doing. While talking about someone's grandfather, for instance, I might be shown someone who is very tall, and get a response like "No my grandfather was short, my uncle was the tall one". The uncle might then start talking, giving messages to his family, the seemingly incorrect information having been given in fact to change the focus of the telepathic conversation to the uncle.

It's as if what I do as a medium is facilitate telepathic conversations, connected mind to connected mind, by getting two people, one dead and one alive, to simultaneously focus on the same thing. The connection that occurs with this simultaneous focusing is the goal. It's what the whole process is about, and what people ultimately find so meaningful. In essence, I'm facilitating a telepathic conversation where one person needs some help and prompting to focus their connected mind. I think the important part of the experience, of any meaningful conversation really, is the telepathic conversation: the actual connection of minds and the shared journey through particular memories, feelings, thoughts, meanings or subtle realities. The words aren't the important part, it's the meanings that are exchanged without using words that are the important part. In other words, in ordinary conversation, words point directly to meaning, whereas with telepathic conversations, meanings are exchanged and words aren't needed. Telepathy is our first language, and while language supports telepathic conversation, and makes it more explicit, it is still once removed from the truly meaningful exchanges that occur telepathically.

It's easy to understand how we came away from our telepathic connection and slowly lost touch with it over time. The explicit and exacting nature of language is very useful for the physical world, and words have their own beauty. Language facilitates complex transactions, barter, trade and negotiation, and written language permits precise communication of incredibly complex stories and concepts through time. Language is useful and beautiful, but it is infinitely more useful when we can acknowledge that language can't fulfil our deeper needs for connection and meaning, and that to truly understand one another or grasp the true meaning of anything, we have to stop talking, even in our own heads, and go beyond words.

Even more than the fact that dead people are still present in our lives, or that they can act like guardian angels for us, what's really interesting about dead people referencing a time when a living person was thinking or talking to them is that the dead person inevitably explains that they were there, and heard everything. The mere act of focusing on a dead person seems to make a connection and open up a channel for telepathic conversation. Our loved ones, their love, and their guidance from a higher perspective are always only a thought away. Most living people can't even acknowledge that it's possible, let alone notice that they're doing it without any effort.

Many of the people who try the hardest to make connections with dead people are grieving, and unable to connect with anyone because of grief. Grief can push us into our survivor minds, cut us off from feeling the comfort of a loved one's presence, and from the possibility of experiencing the telepathic interactions we so badly need. The pain of the loss of a loved one can take people into a place of lack, fear and scarcity – the survivor mind. If you are grieving, I say, keep talking. Your loved ones hear you and they're there whenever you talk to them. Eventually as the grief subsides, or if you are able to align with your love for a departed person, not the grief of their loss, you'll be able to think of them in your connected mind without triggering the loss and start to feel, see or hear their presence for yourself.

When we talk to dead people we might think we are just talking into thin air, or that the conversation is just one way. It's not. When a living person is talking to a dead person out loud, or in their head, there is usually a little bit of a two-way conversation going on, only most people dismiss the return conversation as random thoughts or their imagination. For example, I once had to ask a woman in one of my group sessions about just having talked to her father in her car. A little shocked, she confirmed that she had been talking to her dad while driving days before, and that she knew, but wouldn't dare say, or fully accept, that it was her father who had saved her life by making her slow her car and notice a speeding van that would likely have killed her, had she continued through a green light.

She explained that the entire experience had been surreal and frightening, but she was sure her father was present and made her feel warm, fuzzy and safe: the sensory-symbolic equivalent of "I love you, I'm always here for you, and I got your back." Even though this woman had a strong feeling that her father was still present in her life, and she still talked to him, she couldn't completely let in the notion that she had been having a telepathic conversation in her car, until I brought up the event and confirmed it for her. The experience of feeling warm, fuzzy and safe, and feeling the presence of a loved one is fairly common, especially in times of stress, and in my books, not such a big deal. Your dead people are just saying, "Hi, I love you, and everything's going to be okay," without words.

Whether we are consciously aware or not, we are all having telepathic conversations all the time. Everyone, living or dead, has some ability to receive and perceive ideas through subtle sensory information, as well as impress ideas and subtle sensory-symbolic information onto another person's mind. This process is happening all the time whether you are open to it or not. Most often, we think we are only talking to ourselves, or thinking to ourselves when really some of those thoughts are not our own and have actually been intentionally impressed into our awareness by someone else, or something outside of ourselves. I now see my job as a medium as facilitating telepathic conversations for people who haven't yet developed the ability to consciously conduct a telepathic conversation on their own. I like to point out to people how and where these conversations are already happening in their lives, and teach them how to become conscious of these conversations when they happen. Ultimately, I want to teach people how to consciously have their own experiences so they don't need a medium or telepath for basic interactions anymore.

If you do want to start consciously communicating telepathically with dead people, animals, plants or other beings, you have to be willing to leave your words behind. Animals clearly don't use words, and while dead people can understand words, they don't usually talk back with words. To communicate, you have to do it their way and rely on subtle sensory information. You won't magically start hearing words in your head when you tune into an animal, unless you've already translated subtle sensory information into English unconsciously, which means you've missed a step. Similarly, saying or repeating words in your head while you focus on an animal or other being won't work either, though dead people do seem to hear and understand language in your head, as well as spoken aloud.

Working as a medium, I will occasionally say a phrase, something like "well wasn't that awesome", and have sitters tell me that the phrase was something their dead person said a lot, and that I said it with the same inflection and gestures as their dead person used to say it with. When I do this, I don't really hear the phrase in my head, I just sort of blurt it out; more like a clairiscience, I just know what to say and how to say it. I do also occasionally have dead people show me a word in my head, like it's spelled out on a chalkboard, but it's rare. Even when I'm talking to dead people who understand English, I'm still sharing thought bubbles of subtle sensory information and sentience back and forth – I don't have to say things out loud or in words in my head.

In fact, I'm not entirely convinced that dead people really pay attention to our words when we talk to them; it may be that they perceive the thoughts behind language more than the words. I've never experienced trouble communicating with dead people who didn't speak any English in life. Non-English speakers sometimes share information in reverse order, sort of like the arrangement of verbs and nouns is different in different languages, but I've talked to lots of grandparents – Japanese, German, Filipino – none of whom spoke English in life, and we've communicated just fine without a shared language. Sometimes they've even made me say words in languages I don't speak. It was through these kinds of experiences early on that I came to see that I'm not getting any language in my communications, it's all subtle sensory symbolic communication.

Whether you're talking to dead people, animals, or want psychic information about anything, the first step in telepathic communication is focus. The simple act of focusing on someone or something establishes a telepathic connection. Remember, you are not focusing on the physical person, animal, being, subject or object, or on thoughts or judgements about them or it. You are focusing your connected mind on the idea of them, looking to establish a consciousness to consciousness connection in subtle reality. Physically looking at a person or animal can be a way in, but if you only focus on a person or animal's face or body, you're not establishing a connection in subtle reality, you're just focusing through your eyes onto their physical being. To get to a person's or animal's connected mind and subtle realities, you can start by looking at their physical body or picture it with your eyes, but you then have to shift your focus inward and gently wonder, holding the idea of the person or animal in mind.

Wonder, with gentle curiosity, and be receptive to your subtle senses; you're looking for subtle sensory information, not conceptual language information. You can also think of the process as over identifying as you physically look at a person or animal, and then allowing your connected mind to follow the physical form into the subtle realities behind the physical form. Looking another living person in the eye for an extended period or, more specifically, looking into one another's left eyes with quiet minds for an extended period of time facilitates this process and is a good way to get familiar with the sensation of receiving telepathic information.

Whomever you are telepathically conversing with, once you are focused and have a connection, there are two parts to the equation: (1) perceiving and understanding subtle sensory information; and (2) creating and sending subtle sensory information. Perceiving telepathic information is largely about discernment: the ability to discern very subtle sensory cues; an ability that some of us are naturally good at, and one that can be developed and honed through practice. Discerning subtle differences in taste, sound, feel or vibe in the physical world is a good place to start. You can begin to hone your discernment abilities simply by spending time enjoying and really focusing on music, food, scents, aromas, aesthetics, your body or pretty much anything sensory.

Spending time withdrawing your focus from your physical senses, and 'resetting' your sensory thresholds by focusing only on sensations you experience without physical stimulus, through meditation, clean eating, fasting or similar practices, can enhance the sensitivity of your subtle senses. Understanding the subtle sensory information you do receive is largely a matter of practice, and of developing a subtle sensory vocabulary by correlating the subtle realities you perceive with the physical world. This can be done by spending time in your connected mind in the real world and noticing how your inner experiences correlate with your outer experiences, talking or journaling about your subtle sensory experiences, or through practice actually doing psychic or mediumship readings.

The second part of the telepathic communication equation, sending subtle sensory information, is important and relevant in day to day life, as well as for telepathic communication. As far as telepathic conversations go, know that some dead people are really good at painting detailed sensory scenes and sending the information while others aren't so proficient. How a mediumship session goes depends on the abilities of the dead people you are talking to as well as your own.

Animals aren't oriented in time the way people are, and telepathic conversations with animals don't quite follow a back and forth exchange like telepathic conversations with dead people do. All animals are very telepathic, live in their connected minds, and perceive you and one another through their subtle senses as much as their physical senses. They don't have overly developed survivor minds that constantly keep them out of the present moment by ruminating on the past and future. Present circumstances that are similar to past experiences do, however, trigger animals' memories of past experiences and instinctual drives to inform their behavior in the present moment.

Animals see the images in your head and sense your emotional state very keenly. You don't really need to send animals telepathic information because they're already getting it. It's important to notice that animals keenly pick up on whatever is going on with you. For example, if you have a horse and you go see your horse every day after working at a job you hate, your horse knows all about it. Just by sharing space you share your thoughts, and every feeling you have about those thoughts. My question for you is this: Should your pet really have to deal with your problems? When horse after horse has asked me to ask their person to take responsibility for their energy before they come to the barn, I have to think that subjecting animals to survivor mind stress day after day is really not okay – even if animals help us with our stress, it's at a cost to them.

I've had horses ask me if they are being sold, killed, given away or even dying, because of the thoughts their human has inadvertently over shared. Many horses, even though they're healthy and have a safe and secure home, can get confused, thinking something is actually wrong with them, or something bad is about to happen. Horses that are exposed to their overwhelmed humans' worrisome and unpleasant thoughts take on those confusing and sometimes half-formed thoughts and start to internalize them. Animals react to subtle sensory information as much as, or possibly more than, physical cues, which is why if you're afraid of dogs, you are at a greater risk of getting bitten. Picking up on fear, a fearful dog will react to your fear and bite, much like my brother's experience with anything that has a stinger. It's also why if you're having a problem with your pet or horse, it's probably stemming from you, not them, and your animal's bad behavior or performance is a reflection of your state of mind or an issue in your life.

If you want to have a conscious two-way telepathic connection with an animal, you have to be in a calm, harmless, non-manipulative state of being, sending out good, loving, subtle sensory vibes so that they barely notice you're there, you feel good to them, and you match their vibe or state of being so that they identify you as one of them. If you feel good telepathically, all harmless, fuzzy and loving, animals will naturally want to connect with you telepathically. Some animals, especially larger ones, react to my telepathic connection with a "Holy crap, you can hear me?!" vibe. In some cases, horses (and some dogs) are relieved that their oblivious humans might finally understand them, pay closer attention, and take better care of their wants and needs. I once went to a barn and worked with almost 20 horses who, in the process of discussing other things, each expressed a desire as to which stall they wanted to be in and which horses they wanted near them. After I left, the barn owners moved everyone to their new desired stalls. I received an e-mail the next day that for the first time ever, when the barn owner left the barn for the night, it was totally silent: everyone was content.

When I communicate with animals, typically they methodically share their likes and dislikes, food requests, favorite memories and toys, the emotional state of their human, memories of trips or outings, and questions about other animals or people. You can impress images and ideas to animals simply by imagining a story or idea in your own mind in sensory detail, and actually have a bit of a back and forth conversation with some animals. I often have to confirm for horses where their babies or friends have gone in this way; when a horse is moved to another barn or dies, the remaining horses in a stable, not always privy to what has happened, often bring up questions about where the missing horse has gone.

In my experience, pets are often stressed because they don't understand all the details about what's happening in their home, or what is happening in the lives of their friends and owners.

What they do get is our reactions, thoughts, fears, what ifs, should haves, and feelings about the situation, which can be very confusing and stressful for them. They know something is wrong, but not what, how it affects them, or what they are to do about it. Horses and dogs alike often calm down, and bad behaviors sometimes disappear as soon as I explain to them, with feelings and the pictures in my head, what is going on in their household or barn. Separation anxiety and unwanted behaviors also often disappear when pet owners take some time to share loving, calm feelings with their pets, and share images of what is going on, particularly before leaving for an extended period or for work for the day. Distance doesn't matter, so focusing on your animal and sending them calm loving thoughts throughout the day, or having a caretaker read a loving note to them in your absence, can be very beneficial to your animal: you are always connected.

I find that communicating with living animals is actually much easier than communicating with dead people, and for me, talking to horses is almost as easy as having a regular conversation. Although the connected mind is largely independent of time and distance, and I can telepathically work with people on the other side of the world, talk to dead people who aren't in the physical world at all, as well as communicate with horses across the continent over the phone, it is really easy for me to connect with animals that are right in front of me. I'm not entirely sure if this ease stems from the ease with which horses communicate telepathically, or simple proximity. It's likely the combination I think, since some horses have shown me that they mostly live in their connected minds, and less often as individual personalities. Some horses actually pity our typically egocentric human existence, and the stressed, painfully lonely lives many of us live as a result.

There are some instances for me where working with humans is a little easier in person, and physical contact can open, deepen or change the nature of telepathic connection; touch is a way to focus and you get different information touching people in different ways. I still prefer to work with humans by phone though, largely because it removes the distraction of the physical interaction from the work and forces sitters to focus in their connected minds rather than on our physical interaction. Working by phone also seems to help skeptical sitters open up and participate in the process, as it takes away the possibility that I am using appearance and body language clues to cold read.

Although most humans seem oblivious to subtle sensory information, and most of us talk ourselves out of acknowledging the subtle sensory experiences we do have, humans profoundly affect one another through subtle sensory interactions, all the time. What we tend to refer to as our presence has as much or more to do with the subtle sensory information we are sending out than it does with our physical appearance, words or actions. Our subconscious experience of the world, and even the workings of what has been labeled our subconscious mind, I think, has more to do with subtle sensory interactions than anything in what we might think of as our own individual personal subconscious. Really, we are all having telepathic conversations with one another, unconsciously, all the time, what I refer to as energetic conversations. These conversations often energize, drive or inspire us to action. They determine what's going to happen next in any given interaction as much as our conscious thoughts, intentions and decisions do.

The subtle sensory information we are sending out all the time, our contribution to the subtle sensory conversation and the subtle sensory environment around us, largely depends on our thoughts, emotional state and focus. Being aware of and responsible for the subtle sensory information you send out is a basic courtesy and responsibility that sadly many people lack. I remember Oprah having a quote up in her dressing room that she would regularly refer to: "Please be responsible for the energy you bring into this space." Now if only we could post that all over the planet! Just as a contact high from someone's presence can be totally transformative, your miserable energy can completely deflate others and take their entire day off course.

Becoming aware of your subtle sensory presence is not difficult; it's mostly about accepting the fact that your inner state affects all the beings around you, and noticing your inner state. Being responsible for your energy comes when you accept that you can change your inner state by changing your focus, and doing so whenever you notice that your focus is dragging you and everyone around you down. With time and practice being responsible for your energy, you will gain the ability to consciously impress desired states, ideas and sensations onto telepathically receptive people and animals – a highly useful ability that lets you create the experiences you want in the world, accomplish what you want to accomplish in enjoyable win-win-win ways and express yourself telepathically in two-way telepathic conversations.

Like it or not though, whenever two or more people, animals, or beings come together in physical proximity to one another, unconscious telepathic interactions, or energetic conversations happen. These conversations are where the rubber hits the road, where subtle realities become physical realities. Unconsciously, these conversations can be more like a wrestling match happening at such lightning speed that nobody really knows what just happened. Whenever you suddenly find yourself acting in an unusual way, or saying something unexpectedly, without thinking, those moments when you look back saying, "I don't know what happened, I just found myself…" you've been inspired, energized or driven to speak or act through a subtle reality or a subtle sensory interaction. Something in you has been activated, or triggered, something that, to most people, is mysterious and inexplicable, but we can put a name to: a driver in your subtle reality.

Participated in more consciously and co-creatively, energetic conversations between two people or beings take on a life of their own, synergistically shaping what's going to happen next, so that what does happen next looks like an orchestrated, coordinated dance. Telepathic conversations between living beings can act as a prelude towards such conscious energetic conversations. Verbally aided or not, telepathic conversations that start out with a sort of show and tell where ideas, feelings, and thoughts containing packages of sentience are swapped and can progress to conscious, co-creative conversations in subtle reality. Rather than two people separately thinking and having a verbal conversation, while their consciousnesses tug at one another to determine which subtle realities will play out next, co-creative energetic conversations occur when two or more people come together in subtle reality.

When connected minds intentionally come together to focus in subtle reality, blending possible futures and subtle realities together, they develop new spectrums of possible futures. The process is highly creative because of the synergetic nature of the connected mind: change one tiny element in subtle reality and the entire subtle reality can profoundly change in completely unpredictable and unexpected ways. When connected minds come together, everything changes and possibilities multiply exponentially. As these possibilities are explored, still new possibilities emerge and so on. We think that the real power and potential of the human mind lies in this ability to consciously co-create: to co-create spectrums of beautiful, thrilling, synergistic win-win-win, desired possible futures with awareness and intention in subtle reality, with others, and choose the most desirable scenarios to flow into the physical world.

One of the greatest tragedies in life is people's refusal to participate in the co-creation process. All too often, people choose to remain trapped in narrow ranges of ideas and behavior, and the repeating loops of unfulfilling life experiences that result when we choose to live our lives based solely on the conceptual shoulds, shouldn'ts and judgements of our own survivor mind. In doing so, we are not only holding ourselves back, we are holding everybody else back as well, keeping everyone around us mired in drama and mistrust rather than thriving in inspiration, support and safety. Co-creation only works when everybody involved is tuned in to an evolving collective vision, and willing to let that vision inspire and guide their thoughts and actions. Egos and survivor minds that can't or won't understand or accept people and things as they actually are, and where things are going, can easily gum up any co-creative endeavor with co-dependent drama by playing out their own tiny agendas and insisting that people act and behave only in ways that they think they should.

Ideally, as fully conscious beings, we would live in two realities simultaneously. We would consciously co-create in subtle reality while still being fully present in physical reality. We would consciously participate in telepathic and energetic conversations, and let those conversations inform and inspire our words and actions in the physical world. In other words, we would seamlessly cycle between our bio-minds and connected minds, allowing each to inform, enhance and augment the other. We would understand the consequences and effects of all of our actions in the physical world, before acting, because we would be consciously co-creating and previewing our possible futures with our connected minds in subtle reality all the time, then choosing our actions with wisdom and clairvoyance.

I think many of history's great leaders and visionary founders of companies and movements have been highly skilled in this regard, strongly tuned into an evolving collective vision, and able to speak and act to inspire many people towards the realization of that vision. I also think many people on the planet already do this to varying degrees. Creating a shared vision is standard practice for business people, activists, artists and politicians around the world, though I doubt that they understand the fullness of why this practice is so effective. Many of us intentionally co-create parts of our day, and our lives, whether we are conscious of the process or not, when we set goals or intentions, lose ourselves in the moment, intuitively take a moment to breathe, some quiet time, meditate, pray, or just do something enjoyable for a few minutes. In doing so, we are allowing our connected minds to co-create solutions to problems we can't solve logically, and inspire our thoughts and actions towards the realization of those solutions.

A lot of us intuitively connect with others in the moment, and use that connection to co-create in the moment. At work, we call co-creating in the moment teamwork, synergy or outstanding customer service. At play, we call co-creating fun. We understand co-creative relationships as being *good, true love,* or *real, genuine friendship*. I know that we are collectively getting better and better at consciously co-creating, and our children will be more proficient still. For most people, the most important step is simply becoming aware of and accountable for their telepathic influence on the world. Facilitating this process, helping people bring consciousness to every area of their lives is the bigger part of my job as a telepath: helping people to understand themselves, their place in the universe, the consequences of all of their thoughts, actions and decisions, and how, and in exactly what ways, we are powerful beyond measure.

Fall in love with some activity, and do it! Nobody ever figures out what life is all about, and it doesn't matter. Explore the world. Nearly everything is really interesting if you go into it deeply enough. Work as hard and as much as you want to on the things you like to do the best. Don't think about what you want to be, but what you want to do. Keep up some kind of a minimum with other things so that society doesn't stop you from doing anything at all.
~ Richard Feynman

Notes

1. An extensive body of peer reviewed journal articles is on public record and many articles freely available online. Summaries of the scientific evidence can be found in books such as *Science and Psychic Phenomena: The Fall of the House of Skeptics* by Chris Carter; *The Reality of ESP: A Physicist's Proof of Psychic Abilities* by Russell Targ; or *Supernormal: Science, Yoga, and the Evidence for Extraordinary Psychic Abilities* by Dean Radin.
2. Doing gallery mediumship in front of large groups has taught me that psychically looking for information or people, essentially establishing a connection through which information can flow, is much more difficult and draining than sending and receiving information once a connection is established.
3. Pribram describes the 200-year history of brain research, and his involvement in the field over seven decades, along with his holonomic model of the brain, in his 2013 book, *The Form Within: My Point of View.*
4. Modern medicine is beginning to recognize that the brain is not a machine, or a hardwired computer, and is remarkably resilient, as well as capable of miraculous recovery and change. Works such as *The Brain That Changes Itself,* a New York Times bestseller by Norman Doidge, explore the science of neuroplasticity, case histories of amazing recoveries from brain damage, and (some of) the profound implications of brains that are capable of changing themselves.
5. Karl H. Pribram (2013) *The Form Within: My Point of View,* p. 30.
6. A demonstration of a similar effect can be produced with a slide projector and eyeglasses. If the lens is taken out of a projector, and eyeglasses held up close to the screen, the

image being projected will appear under each lens of any number of eyeglasses held up to the screen. In the case of holographs split into pieces, each piece will generate the holograms recorded on the film, but each hologram will appear at a slightly different angle of view.

7. Identifying similar images using holographic image processing techniques is instant: overlaid holographic interference patterns become brighter the more similar two images are, and darker the more dissimilar – regardless of the location of similarities and the surrounding details of the images being compared. Comparing photographic images by comparing parts of different images to one another, one at a time, requires an immense amount of information processing, and is a difficult task, even for today's powerful computers.
8. Galileo was condemned by the Catholic Church and died under house arrest for sharing the idea that the earth revolves around the sun. The irony of John Maddox, former editor of *Nature*, publicly condemning Rupert Sheldrake by comparing him to Galileo, is that Galileo was correct, and the comparison puts Maddox in the role of the Church. Galileo was publicly pardoned by the Church in 1992, 359 years after he was condemned. Hopefully it won't take so long for history to repeat itself and mainstream science to pardon Rupert.
9. Bohm also referred to the holomovement as the implicate order, and the physical world as the explicate order. His theories are outlined in his 1980 book *Wholeness and the Implicate Order*.
10. General relativity and quantum field theory, the two theories upon which all modern physics rests, have yet to be fully combined into one theory that fully explains all aspects of the universe. Quantum theory doesn't explain gravity, and general relativity, though very successful in explaining

gravity and the behavior of very large objects like stars and galaxies, doesn't explain the behavior of molecules, atoms and subatomic particles. String theory accommodates both quantum field theory and general relativity, but it is not yet possible to experimentally test the predictions string theory makes about the universe because the energies required far exceed what today's existing technology can generate.

11. In my experience, most of us do unconsciously repeat patterns and unconscious programming through much of our lives. Understanding, embracing and using our connected minds can allow us to recognize and break these patterns and make conscious, meaningful and informed decisions about our lives.
12. Stuart Hameroff and Roger Penrose (2013) "Consciousness in the universe: A review of the 'Orch OR' theory." *Physics of Life Reviews*, 11 (1) pp. 39–78. DOI:10.1016/j.plrev.2013.08.002.
13. S. Sahu; S. Ghosh; K. Hirata; D. Fujita; A. Bandyopadhyay (2013) "Multi-level memory-switching properties of a single brain microtubule." *Appl Phys Lett*, 102, pp. 123701.1–4.
14. Non-computable information processing, if anything, should deepen concerns over unintended consequences of artificial intelligence (AI). Separated from the natural world by design, the presumed 'intelligence' and functioning of AI systems may be very different from the biological neural networks they are intended to mimic or replace and the potential interactions of consciousness of such systems bring a new level of complexity to issue.
15. The statistical probability that the experimental results were observed by chance, the p value, was 0.00000000001%. To be fair, some critics of the PEAR studies suggest that the mind-matter effects are statistical illusions, and disappear through meta-analysis of the data. Some of the assumptions and methods employed in critical meta-analyses, such as

omitting selective portions of data are, however, questionable; see: Radin, D. (2006) "Assessing the Evidence for Mind-Matter Interaction Effects." *Journal of Scientific Exploration*, Vol. 20, No. 3, pp. 361–374.

16. Sexual orientation was not controlled for in the PEAR experiments to our knowledge, and I would guess that the effect would be the same with same sex attraction.
17. Christine A. Skarda and Walter J. Freeman, "Chaos and the New Science of the Brain." *Concepts in Neuroscience*, Vol. 1, No. 2 (1990), pp. 275–285.
18. Baruss, I. (August 2014) "A Vision for the Society for Consciousness Studies." *Journal of Consciousness Exploration & Research*, Volume 5, Issue 6, pp. 551–555.
19. Rollin McCraty; Mike Atkinson; and Raymond Trevor Bradley (April 2004) "Electrophysiological Evidence of Intuition: Part 2. A System-Wide Process?" *The Journal of Alternative and Complementary Medicine*, 10(2), pp. 325–336.
20. You can be in your connected mind and bring a timely, respectful and fitting end to another life, as hunters have since the dawn of time. In my experience, humans are the only beings on the planet that fear and resist a timely death that benefits the greater whole, and prefer to wither into decrepitude and physical suffering rather than leave our physical bodies with timely grace.
21. I say "links" rather than "caused" because causality in the connected mind is a very tricky subject. We ordinarily assume that time is strictly linear, an assumption that has consistently proven to be not altogether true in my work. The connected mind exists outside of time, and therefore things in the connected mind can cause multiple events through time, that also affect one another.
22. I say this out of personal experience; further reading on the subject can be found in texts such as *The Cosmic Serpent: DNA and the Origins of Knowledge* by Jeremy Narby or *Mind Trek* by

Joe McMoneagle.

23. This is why the simple act of bringing consciousness to your drivers, which exist in subtle reality, can be profoundly life changing. By bringing your consciousness to your subtle realities and drivers, you change them.
24. Jon Plantania, PhD (2011) *Jung for Beginners*.
25. I use the term *create* very loosely with respect to subtle realities. At some level, subtle realities are like platonic forms, they are universal and ideal, building blocks that are not so much created as they are put together and shared between many people, and through time over moments, generations and millennia.
26. Nancy Segal's *Born Together – Reared Apart* (2012) provides a history of a 25-year long University of Minnesota study of twins reared apart and the personal histories of some of the 137 pairs of twins involved in the study.
27. Christakis, NA and Fowler, JH (2009) *Connected: The Surprising Power of Our Social Networks and How They Shape Our Lives – How Your Friends' Friends' Friends Affect Everything You Feel, Think, and Do*, p. 28.
28. The logical conclusion materialist scientists take from this correlation is that the ability to remember others, and therefore consider them to be part of one's social group, is dictated by the size of the bio-computer inside the brains of primates. The other possible conclusion from this observation is that the complexity of our minds, which are not in our brains, relates to the number and breadth of our telepathic connections, and that this depth and complexity is reflected in the size of the antennas in our skulls that connect our nonphysical minds to our physical bodies.
29. Nicholas Taleb, author, Professor of Risk Engineering at New York University Polytechnic School of Engineering and scientific adviser to the International Monetary Fund. Facebook.

30. Jacob D. Bekenstein (April 1, 2007) "Information in the Holographic Universe: Theoretical results about black holes suggest that the universe could be like a gigantic hologram." *Scientific American*.

6th Books investigates the paranormal, supernatural, explainable or unexplainable. Titles cover everything included within parapsychology: how to, lifestyles, beliefs, myths, theories and memoir.

If you have enjoyed this book, why not tell other readers by posting a review on your preferred book site? Recent bestsellers from 6th Books are:

The Afterlife Unveiled
What the Dead Are Telling Us About Their World!
Stafford Betty
What happens after we die? Spirits speaking through mediums know, and they want us to know. This book unveils their world…
Paperback: 978-1-84694-496-3 e-book: 978-1-84694-926-5

Spirit Release
Sue Allen
A guide to psychic attack, curses, witchcraft, spirit attachment, possession, soul retrieval, haunting, deliverance, exorcism and more, as taught at the College of Psychic Studies.
Paperback: 978-1-84694-033-0 e-book: 978-1-84694-651-6

I'm Still With You
True Stories of Healing Grief Through Spirit Communication
Carole J. Obley
A series of after-death spirit communications which uplift, comfort and heal, and show how love helps us grieve.
Paperback: 978-1-84694-107-8 e-book: 978-1-84694-639-4

Advanced Psychic Development
Becky Walsh
Learn how to practise as a professional, contemporary spiritual medium.
Paperback: 978-1-84694-062-0 e-book: 978-1-78099-941-8

Astral Projection Made Easy
Overcoming the Fear of Death
Stephanie June Sorrell
From the popular Made Easy series, *Astral Projection Made Easy* helps to eliminate the fear of death, through discussion of life beyond the physical body.
Paperback: 978-1-84694-611-0 e-book: 978-1-78099-225-9

The Miracle Workers Handbook
Seven Levels of Power and Manifestation of the Virgin Mary
Sherrie Dillard
Learn how to invoke the Virgin Mary's presence, communicate with her, receive her grace and miracles and become a miracle worker.
Paperback: 978-1-84694-920-3 e-book: 978-1-84694-921-0

Divine Guidance
The Answers You Need to Make Miracles
Stephanie J. King
Ask any question and the answer will be presented, like a direct line to higher realms... *Divine Guidance* helps you to regain control over your own journey through life.
Paperback: 978-1-78099-794-0 e-book: 978-1-78099-793-3

The End of Death
How Near-Death Experiences Prove the Afterlife
Admir Serrano
A compelling examination of the phenomena of Near-Death Experiences.
Paperback: 978-1-78279-233-8 e-book: 978-1-78279-232-1

Less Incomplete
A Guide to Experiencing the Human Condition Beyond the Physical Body
Sandie Gustus
Based on 40 years of scientific research, this book is a dynamic guide to understanding life beyond the physical body.
Paperback: 978-1-84694-351-5 e-book: 978-1-84694-892-3

The Psychic & Spiritual Awareness Manual
A Guide to DIY Enlightenment
Kevin West
Discover practical ways of empowering yourself by unlocking your psychic awareness, through the Spiritualist and New Age approach.
Paperback: 978-1-78279-397-7 e-book: 978-1-78279-396-0

Find more titles and sign up to our readers' newsletter at http://www.johnhuntpublishing.com/mind-body-spirit

Follow us on Facebook at https://www.face-book.com/OBooks and Twitter at https://twitter.com/obooks

Most titles are published in paperback and as an e-book. Paperbacks are available in physical bookshops. Both print and e-book editions are available online. Readers of e-books can click on the live links in the titles to order.